To Virginia & Howard

    Long time friends. All
the best.

Susan "Sam" LeGree

       12-25-05

Champagne in a Plastic Glass

by
Susan "Sam" LeGree

authorHOUSE™

1663 LIBERTY DRIVE, SUITE 200
BLOOMINGTON, INDIANA 47403
(800) 839-8640
WWW.AUTHORHOUSE.COM

First published by AuthorHouse 06/28/05

ISBN: 1-4208-6064-X (sc)

Printed in the United States of America
Bloomington, Indiana

This book is printed on acid-free paper.

Cover photo by Susan "Sam" LeGree.

From The Writer

I feel certain I will never finish my memoir in all its detail. When I began to compile this collection of thoughts and experiences into book form, it came to me that what I had written, in actuality was a memoir. So instead, I offer this collection of thoughts; a lifetime in three parts that flow into one.

People read autobiographies and memoirs because there exists for some, an insatiable appetite to know what another person's life was about; what made them tick. For many it is out of curiosity centered on the famous, infamous, renowned, the accomplished, the privileged, the celebrity. Those perhaps, very much unlike oneself. In the reading however, we delight in the discovery of similar thoughts, beliefs and experiences.

I don't qualify for any of the above reasons to arouse anyone's curiosity. I write because I think there are many more reasons for the ordinary person to write about his or herself. Some people write for an expected profit, along with the thrill of being published. Some simply wish to leave a legacy for their families. Others may write as a method of purging their souls, finding it helpful in working through life's unresolved mysteries and perhaps even exorcising some personal demons in the process.

That last point appeals to me and is a large part of why I am doing this. But greater still is an egotistical desire for a certain continuity of self. What of all the knowledge one gleans throughout a lifetime? What of the life-lessons learned? Why do we strive to know, to feel and to experience, to accomplish, at whatever level, if at the end of one's life all is extinguished without a trace?

Those questions moved me to write this book. Most probably few will care. But just maybe it will endure for a long time. Someone may find it on a trash heap or tucked away in a dusty attic years from now, and will salvage it. Hopefully this person will be like me; someone who is curious to know the heart and soul of a person from the past, and fee! a kinship, thereby bringing her into the present.

Susan "Sam" LeGree
2005

Acknowledgments

I am grateful to the following people who gave me the courage by gently nudging me to publish this book.

Betty Johnston and Carol Kolinsky, my longtime penpals whose every letter to me said, "write, write, write."

Phil Moriarty, an author friend, who continues well into his nineties, to write his thoughts every day. "Go, go!"

Golden Ponds residents, who planted the idea in my mind. "You should publish this."

Joe LeGree my husband, and self-professed biggest fan. "You write, I'll cook."

Contents

IS THAT ALL THERE IS?

When I was young there was a popular song recorded by Peggy Lee, titled "*Is That All There Is?*" The lyrics ask that question in bemused retrospect of a life that perhaps never lives up to full expectation.

My mother, who possessed wonderful insight, told me that when first she heard that song, and ever after, it brought me to her mind.

It is true that I have drunk deeply of life's sweet champagne and I have danced. But forever, I've used the plastic glass of reality and circumstance. Champagne often spills when one keeps on dancing...

REMEMBERING

I was asked how I remember so much over so many years. I remember through my senses, far more than from words read or written long ago.

Memories come through sweetness and bitterness on my tongue, and with the penetrating decibel of sound in my ears that a familiar melody   sends inward to rend my heart.

A scent, at times, can lift me up and carry me back for miles and years in time. A cooling breeze that lifts my hair and a crunch of leaves underfoot awakens sensation of touch that my mind and body thought forever lost.

My sight is not so keen now, but my mind's eye has captured it all.

The senses jog the memory and bring the past forward without bidding.

LIFE SPAN

A nineteenth century mind
thrust into a twentieth century life,
now trespasses upon the
twenty-first century.

A ROSE BY ANY OTHER NAME

Have you ever thought about people's names? Everybody has one or more. There are people who absorb their name so completely that it saturates them. If you meet another person with the same name, you don't notice the coincidence.

Ordinary and not so ordinary names can take on a certain aura when connected with some one you know well, some one you love, some one who is a part of who you are yourself. Family names are like that.

I have an aunt with the lyrical name of Andrie and though she tried, I will never allow her to shorten it to Ann. My brother's middle name was in deference to her, only it was spelled Andre. Another aunt was named Frances. I like that, but somehow she was forever known as Dot.

As for the uncles, Frank was Bud, and Dick, whose real name was John, was always called Pete. My dad, Herbert, borrowed his older brother Bill's birth certificate in order to work in a factory at a too young age. Hence he became Bill.

It was all right with Bill the first, because he and my aunt Stella became Bill-n-Stella.

When mom married dad, she became Cookie, which was derived from the last name, which was Cook. Agnes Livinia was long forgotten, even when she remarried years later and her acquired name was nearly unpronounceable.

I have a nephew who was named Myron. On his sixteenth birthday he asked as a present, to have it legally changed to William. Now there is Bill the third.

2

When I was born I was named Carol, for my mother's nurse. Dad's response to that was, that I "would always be Susan" to him. Most everyone calls me Sam now.

MY SEARCH

Forever trying to find myself,
One day at last, I did.
And I wasn't even there.

MY BIG BROTHER -
May 29,1930 -- July 6, 2004

Today my brother passed away.
I cannot picture myself
Without him, nor this world.

We, the world and I,
Lost a large source of
Laughter, and love.

My brother has been one of the few constants in my life. He was my hero when I was a little girl and my hero still.

Every time I have fallen, my brother has been there, never judging, never criticizing. Just there, and always the same. I have never heard him voice an opinion on anyone's faults or shortcomings. Nor have I ever heard him boast about himself. He has always been a steady, decent man with a playful, teasing nature and a large appetite for adventure and fun.

WRITE SPEAK

One day I overheard
Him speak of me
With pride.

Nothing has ever
Been more rewarding

TO DAD

Whenever I visited you
I felt better
Even though I never
Talked of
What troubled me.

MY FATHER - Jan. 26, 1911 - July 1, 1991

Dad took his tiny, dark-haired girl with him everywhere, leaving mother and brother behind. We often went fishing in his small rowboat with my name painted across her stern, or shared cold watermelon in the park.

He strummed an old banjo and sang with me, and he taught me to click rhythm on a pair of ebony "bones." And he answered my childish questions with an orange for the sun and an apple-earth, to explain the universe.

He demanded that I be as fastidiously groomed as he was himself. When in his presence I was expected to be clean and neatly dressed. He was delighted when my mother arranged and pinned my hair in what he called an up-sweep.

As much as I adored him, I feared him. He never physically harmed me in any way, but his disapproval could reduce me to a quivering mass. I feared him and I feared displeasing him. It seemed I always did both.

His lectures in the basement, with his shiny, black eyes penetrating the very mirror image of them, could wound me more severely and lastingly, than any blow of his hand.

There were occasions when he tried to educate or enlighten me with knowledge that was beyond my years and capabilities. If I did not grasp what he was teaching, a panic would fill my mind and leap to my stomach like a thousand butterflies.

It then became impossible for me to understand anything he said. My mind would shut down and all there was left to know, was that I was not meeting his expectations. And so, I pretended to understand, until I could make my escape.

When I was eleven years old, my father called me into his room one early evening and told me to sit on the bed. He was rifling through dresser drawers and handing me a dozen treasures. A large pair of metal dice that he had made, and a tiny blown-glass bottle with a shiny penny inside - Odd little things that a man collects.

Then he told me he was going away and never would be back. I was told not to cry. I was never allowed to cry.

After he was gone, I cried for a very long time. This was my very first heartbreak and one that affected the rest of my life.

TEARS

A mystery to myself, is
Why do my tears
Flow readily
With my happiness,
And dry when I am sad?

MY MOTHER -- Oct. 2, 1906 -- Nov. 15, 1980

The best part about my mother was the way she viewed the world. She loved the sun and the rain, the dark and the light. She was intrigued by nature and all its plants and creatures. She knew the names of all the trees and flowers, and she always had a garden.

She was kind and humorous. She spoke in never-ending clichés, and made friends effortlessly. She was ever young at heart as she splashed barefoot through puddles left by the rain. She was there with "down home" cooking and hugs and Band-Aids, when needed.

My mother unreservedly adored my brother. He was the son of her greatest love and carried the male genes of his father. His big brother teasing of me at time approached near cruelty.

Being so much older and larger, he hurt me physically at times. Worse, were the times he crushed my fragile self-esteem. I forgave him always, and loved him just as our mother did.

She and I were close, however. Especially during the years when my brother was away in the Army and dad had long ago left us. We entertained each other with our similar sense of humor. I would reduce her to gasping tears of laughter with my antics. Even as I grew taller than she was, I continued to cuddle on her lap and enjoy the warmth and sweet scent of her. I have mostly fond memories of my childhood, mainly due to her.

PUDDLE JUMPERS

When the rain stops,
Take off your shoes,
Little girl
And come with me.

Let's wade through
The puddles,
So I can be
A child, like you.

GOING FOR A WALK

A walk with her
Was brisk between
The many stops
Pull a weed,
Smell a flower,
Listen to a bird's call.

Hello to a neighbor,
Linger for a chat
Retrieve a child's toy
And rescue an insect.

Point out images
In the clouds.
Examine closely
A leaf or stone.

And follow a
Butterfly back home.

LIFE OF THE PARTY

The first name on the guest list
Her presence assured a good time.
Her smiling face, quick wit and
Ready laugh, filled the
Room with good times
And good will.

Never in a boisterous way,
But as comfort and joy
Sometimes enfold one
In its arms,
Without awareness
Of its arrival.

COME SEE THE FLOWERS

She loved to show
Her flower garden
Caressing each bloom
And telling its name.

It seems to me
They returned her pride
With the ultimate that
They could give.

A MOTHER MISSING

Alzheimer's and a series of
Small strokes stealthily crept in
And slowly robbed her
Of her soul.

All that made her funny
And caring,
Naughty and sweet,
Loving and loved.

What was a unique woman,
Became a little, empty shell
That sometimes laughed and
Sometimes cried, about nothing
Anyone else could
Comprehend.

TRYING TO SEE YOU

It haunts me.
The memory of you
In that place where you
Retreated from the world.

I see the image of a
Face no longer yours.
The sparkle in soft
Brown eyes
No longer there.

The smile, a sort of reflex
Worse, the silent tears.
What did they mean?
As you stared back at me.

Were you glad to
See me, sad because
You couldn't speak?
Was there still love
For me?

Did you know me at all,
Or even see me?

GRANDMOTHER DAISY -
Oct. 1880 -- May 9,1943

It was the perfect name for her. Daisy was fresh as springtime, small and dainty. She could blend in a bouquet of humanity, or stand alone in her beauty. The cool, relentless winds of her lifetime, would mercilessly buffet and scatter the petals of her soul. Along the way, she soared and danced in those very winds.

As a child she traveled west with her German immigrant parents where they ran a pony ranch. Probably this is when her love of horses began.

Sometime after the family had settled into their ranching life, a band of hostile Indians from a nearby reservation, for reasons only they will ever know, killed Martin and Elizabeth, and Daisy was an orphan.

In her youth, Daisy found employment as an actress and a bareback rider in a traveling circus. Her blonde good looks and spirited nature opened both doors, and the hearts of men to her.

The circumstances of her time erased all further opportunity to ride a prancing steed with a spotlight illuminating her golden hair and adding sparkle to her blue eyes.

Daisy's life turned to one of hard work, the bearing of six children, and two failed marriages. Hers was the era of W.W.I, and the demanding sacrifices of the great depression. To care for her children, she worked in a glass factory, grateful for the income.

When I was about seven years old, and she seemed ancient, she came with her cats, to share a room with me. She passed away before my young eyes, while I held the pieces of fabric she was weaving into a rug.

Her life, like the rug, was put aside; never truly finished.

FOREVER YOUNG

The only way not to age
Is to live in the
Memory of another

SUMMERTIME AND THE LIVIN' WAS EASY

Like most children, I counted the days until summer vacation from school. What a dreamy time of softball and roller skating and catching lightning bugs in a jar.

Going barefoot was a rite of summer and you did so despite the scorching sidewalks that burned and the pebbles that pierced your tender feet, before they acquired their summer callous.

Did you ever go out after dark with a flashlight and a tin can to pull earthworms from the dewy grass? That meant fishing early the next morning.

Homes in my modest neighborhood did not have swimming pools. Whenever our parents watered the lawn and flowers with the garden hose, kids appeared from everywhere to play in the refreshing stream of water.

Summer was special. It offered its own agenda from bicycling to lying on one's back in the grass, making imaginary pictures from the ever changing clouds.

We had no car and we never went away on a vacation. That is something I never realized that we lacked.

A twelve inch black and white television made its way into our living room when I was a bit older, but I only looked at it when I had to come in after dark.

The days were filled with friends, playing and romping, with our dogs happily tagging along like shadows.

Dogs at that time ran loose and never made routine calls at a veterinarian. No fancy titles or registry, they were just dogs.

Occasionally we put on our shoes, slicked our hair and attended a summer-birthday party. Birthday parties were not held at Chuck-E-Cheese or a pizza parlor with video games.

They were held in our homes. Moms made a birthday cake with candles, we played games like dropping wooden clothes pins into a milk bottle. What is a clothes pin and a milk bottle? The kids today might well ask.

There were prizes to the winners of the games; brightly wrapped little gifts, and ice cream to go along with the birthday cake.

The delicacies of summer fare are a subject of their own. Watermelon, corn on the cob, green apples and strawberry shortcake that mom made from dough, not those awful little round sponge cakes you find today. Ice cream often was homemade. The finest I have ever tasted to this day, was that made by a neighbor from home grown sweet peaches.

Before long, the "Ice Cream Man" entered our summer world. They peddled a tricycle-type vehicle with a large square container in which dry ice kept the treats frozen. Ice cream bars, push-ups, popsicles and more. The various-sized bells mounted on the handlebars of the vendor's vehicle could be heard several blocks away, sending kids scrambling in the house for change.

As I remember those childhood summers, with long, imaginative play, I realize that they were as important to our mental growth as the book learning days of school that inevitably followed.

BACK TO SCHOOL

Where I grew up, "back to school" happened in September, just after Labor Day. My birthday, late in August always signaled the imminent fact that summer vacation was ending and the school year was about to begin. Also, my birthday gifts were mostly school clothes.

The annual downtown shopping trip for a new winter coat was quick to follow. It seems I was never able to wear the same coat for a second year, since my arms and legs kept lengthening. Mom would often buy a coat that was a bit long for me, with the hope that by the following year it would fit just right. It never happened.

As if the post birthday and all it signified wasn't bad enough, my world would suddenly and dramatically morph itself into autumn. The air felt different … crisper. The leaves began turning color overnight, and to cover the sidewalks, so that I could no longer roller skate.

As if taunting me, the locusts would set up their buzz saws and fill the late afternoon stillness with their orchestrations. Their droning would build and build to a crescendo, then suddenly stop as if their leader had dropped his baton.

My bicycle chain would be broken and the metal wheels of my skates were worn through to the ball bearings. It was time to put childish things aside.

GOOD QUESTION

Once when I was
Quite grown,
and working in
my office, a little boy
Wandered in and asked,
What I wanted to be
When I grew up.

I don't think
I could answer,
Even if asked today,
As I never knew, nor
Did I ever grow up.

EVERYBODY TALKS ABOUT THE WEATHER

Have you noticed, as I have, that as life goes on we become more interested in the weather? We hang up inside/outside thermometers and rain gauges. Some of us even mount sophisticated barometers on the wall. I never could figure out how to read those.

The first thing I look at in the morning newspaper is the upper right corner of the front page, to see the weather forecast for the day. I have a good idea what it will say, since I just came inside from the rain, after crawling around on the wet, cold ground retrieving the paper from under the car or behind the bushes. Dressed in my nightie, with curlers covering my head, this is not a pretty sight at 6:00 A.M.

On the back of the sports pages is a complete run down of everything you would ever want to know about the weather worldwide. You get yesterday's high and low temperatures as well as today's and tomorrow's. Transplanted Floridians always check out their northern hometown so they can gloat a little, especially in the winter.

Later in the day, when the television is turned to the news, everything comes to a standstill when the weather person comes on. Why are we so interested anyway, when we just have to take it as it comes?

The Hurricane Season is worth noting for sure. We all breathe a sigh of relief when November comes around and we've not lost our happy homes. Except for that extreme, what is there to talk about? In Florida the summer is hot and hotter. It either rains or it doesn't. Usually it rains when we don't need any and doesn't rain when we do. I just keep my umbrella handy and watch for the rainbows.

My mother was a good weather forecaster. If her knees hurt it was going to rain. If the clouds looked like a mackerel's scales, or were wispy horses tails; a change was coming. If there was a red setting sun at night, it was a sailor's delight.

Oh well, there will be weather, whether or not.

THE FOUR SEASONS

Spring: The earth awakens from a long silent sleep, as if
born anew.
A baby is born and begins to grow - to live.

Summer: The earth is wide-awake, lovely with beckoning
adventure.
The child has grown to youthful maturity. He laughs, loves,
and becomes.

Autumn: The earth's beauty and ambition begins to fail,
though it
Desperately tries to keep them.
The child is not a child now, but has reached middle age.
The time hastens and he begins to lose his beauty
and strength of youth.

Winter: The earth dies away again, to be born anew come
spring.
The man dies and is laid to rest eternally in
the bosom of the earth.

Never more will he see and smell the freshness of spring,
The gaiety of summer, nor the faltering of autumn.
Only the still, restfulness of winter.

JANUARY ICE

I have to watch you, January,
My eyes upon the ground.
I walk with footsteps wary,
Lest you turn me upside down

SLEET

Waiting for the bus
One early day,
For delivery to
My workplace

I stood in high-heeled
Shoes beneath an
Umbrella grown
Heavy with ice.

How forlorn I must have
Appeared,
As ice cycles caged
Me in,
While I shivered.

The bus was behind
Schedule, and
So was I

The boss; high, dry,
And mighty, asks
"Where have you been?"

1965

Susan *"Sam" LeGree*

APRIL FOOL!

Trees were budding
And the breeze
Was warm today.

Tomorrow - I awoke to
A world turned white.

It was April first.

RAIN

I have a love-hate
Relationship with the rain.
To awaken early to
the patter of drops
upon the roof,
Is soothing.
And cozy. I love it.

But sometimes it wears
Out its welcome
As it lasts throughout the day
And the sky stays gray.

I hate the darkness
It brings.

TOO EARLY FOR CHRISTMAS

I am what is known as a
"Christmas person." Age never
diminishes my enthusiasm and
pure joy in the season.

However, I also think Halloween
Decorations and celebrations
Are fun.
And what about Thanksgiving?

What a festive and meaningful
Time of year, is that.

My question; why must the
Great world of retail
Whisk us past Halloween
And Thanksgiving
So fast?

FALL IS COMING

A faint stirring of the senses
Like that which sways
The tree tops.
It's around the corner,
Like wisps of scented smoke
In the air
Reaching around to wrap you
In a filmy cloak.

It's following closely
At your heels,
In swirling dust-devils,
And over there,
Peeking at you, are apples
Red as the roses were

It will be here soon,
To tap you on the nose
And chill your bones.
But gently, and with
A frosty smile.

A LEAF IN THE WIND

Gaily swirling in mad convulsions
Of blazing color,
Now lazily drifting, drifting,
Almost ceasing to fall.

Leaves upon the ground,
Brown and dry and lifeless;
Completely at the mercy of
Whimsical winds that
Catch them and fling them
Skyward once more.

Like these falling leaves of autumn,
My life is fashioned.
So be it, if it is destined.
I've seen the autumn, I've watched
Its glorious struggle,
And I've seen it graciously lose.

I've marveled at it
Consumed by its power.
I've basked in its presence,
Asking only that I may do so,
Seeing all the while
Its tinge of death.

Ignoring it, I've looked only
At its beauty,
The undemanding, rightfulness
Of its being,
Sat back and awaited
Its ending.

SCENTS AND SENSES

If it weren't for our senses, there would probably be no memory. Since both our senses and our memory weaken a bit as the years go by, I think we can appreciate how one can jog the other.

Sight, sound, taste, touch and smell have the miraculous power to transfer one back to childhood. What fun that can be, for however long it will last.

What a feast for the eyes when the cards and wrapping paper, ribbons and shiny ornaments, suddenly appear in the stores. The neighborhood lights and other decorations spring forth shortly after (or before) the Thanksgiving leftovers are gone.

Who hasn't walked by a Christmas tree lot and deeply breathed in the scent of pine? That can really take you back! And if you are fortunate enough to have someone in your house who is baking cookies, what a heavenly aroma fills the air. If there is no one to bake, then why not you?

We always had a large bowl of tangerines and oranges in our house during the holiday season. Forever after, the scent of citrus makes me feel about six years old.

The sounds of Christmas are the best ... from off-key caroling to the Salvation Army's clanging bells. Best of all is when the voice of a stranger wishes you a merry Christmas, and happy holidays.

There was a man who worked in the business world downtown, when I was there. I will never forget him, though I never knew who he was. Every December, as he passed us people on the streets, he offered a handshake, and left a candy cane in our hand.

Christmas season turns me into a cookie baking fanatic. Out come the mixer and cookie cutters for their once a year performance. Magazines and newspapers are full of holes, where recipes once were. The kitchen floor and counters are snow-covered in flour and sugar.

All these things and so many more, bring the memories flowing. They have the ability to wrap me in a warm swirl of good thoughts, kindly thoughts, childish thoughts.

Every year brings back the old and presents the future memories.

CHRISTMAS PAST

Fragrant spikes of green
In the most remote of places.
The doorbell has gone mute.

How bleak the rooms,
How large they've grown.
The mailman arrives
Unnoticed.

I read somewhere, that a writer should never throw old attempts away, no matter how embarrassing. Here are some of mine:

FIND ME

Located halfway between a
Singing smile, and
Two dancing feet,
If you will only take time
To notice, there is me.

A heart that lies in waiting,
To leap upon the
Promise of you
And to break a little more,
When you turn away.

22

I speak to you, love.
Look between my happy song
And rhythmic shoes,
To see me.

And come to me soon,
Lest I run out of
Songs to sing,
And I dance too far away.

1962

SHORT VISIT

Oh love, you child's dream,
You maker of bliss,
Yet breaker of the heart.
You divest all within
Your gleam, when
Your prodigies impart.

Oh love, you breach of trust
You promise-kept
Of ecstasy, and yet
Infidel of the heart.
You come and swiftly
Turn to dust.
But ever leave your mark.

Oh love, you pompous loan
You sweet sample
Of death,
Yet substance of the heart.
You shout your presence known,
Then whisper your depart.

UNFULFILLED PROMISE

Sweet gemmule, in the heat
Of spring-kissed
You must burst from your
Cloak of sanctity.

You thrust your fullest bloom,
Eager to the mist,
And drink deeply its ecstasy.

But what now, little flower,
That you have drunk
your fill?
You know not if again
You'll meet.

You stand alone,
In winds grown still.
Head bent, fragrant petals
at your feet.

WILL EVERYTHING BE MINE?

When a new experience is mine
Or in a better place I've dined,
I always think, "this is it, now
Everything is mine."

When I travel to a new site,
By bus, by train, in flight -
I always think, "I can stop, now
All was in my sight."

Or when I touch on sweet lips
And wines have come in sips,
I always think, "I'm through, now
All good has found my lips."

But there's always more to be mine
Seems that's life's incline.
So I cannot say, "It's over, now"
Only death can make
That mine.

REMEMBERING YOU

Once you asked me
How I'll remember you.
I didn't choose to answer,
Until I thought it through.

I know now, I'll remember
By everything around.
From long rides in the country
To the bright lights of town.

I'll remember you in morning
When birds sing to the sun,
And in the warmth of darkness,
After day is done.

I'll remember you always
In happiness, and caring.
In gentle talk, and lonely walks,
And through the joy of sharing.

Many things will bring to mind
The private smiles, and laughter.
Memories of times we've shared
Will live forever after.

For as long as I am living
You shall be living too.
I'll remember you in all things
For all my world, was you.

1965

NOTHING

Do you know what nothing is?
I have come to know.
It is the loss of all things,
With nowhere to go.

WINDOW VIEW

From my window
I have seen the robins leave.
I've watched the squirrels at work,
And heard the pigeons grieve.

From that same window,
I've seen the trees turn gold.
I've watched snow cover all,
And heard the wind blow bold.

From the window
I have seen flowers sprout.
I've watched spring's showers
And heard the fountain spout.

And, from my window,
I've seen my love appear.
I've watched for his arrival,
And heard his footsteps near.

From my window
We've seen the sky above.
and watched the stars appear,
As we whispered words of love.

Now, at my window
I'm seen most every day,
Watching the ever-changing scene,
Since I watched him walk away.

1965

DROWNING

I am going down. I am drowning
And it is suicidal.
For rescue is close at hand.
A drowning man will grasp at a straw
While I ignore the nearby floating logs
Of truth and intelligence.

The life preserver of good and
Righteousness is the
Extended hands of friendship
And love.

I can not swim I am not strong.
Perhaps I would float,
If I could but relax and
care enough to try.

But no, instead I close my eyes
To salvation.
I open my mouth wide,
To swallow the sea
Of self-destruction.

LAST LAUGH

You broke your word,
Your vows, and the law.
You only bruised my pride.
You couldn't break my heart,
Because I never loved you.

HAPPY IS AS HAPPY DOES

I have never wallowed in self-pity for long.
That is what loneliness is, much of the time,
And so is boredom.

I've always been able to pick myself up,
Accept what is, and go about adapting
to that which will make me
as whole as possible.

I love life just for the shear
Joy of living it.
I guess when you feel that way,
It is impossible to be unhappy
For too long a time.

FIRST FLIGHT

Today I've seen something
I've never seen before;
The other side of the clouds.
They were thick, fluffy cotton
And where the sun touched,
Like mounds of pristine snow.

At first they were but wisps,
Smoke-like
Over a neat patchwork quilt.

Later they grew dense and
There was nothing below
But endless white,
And above, infinite sky.

MAGICAL MOMENTS

What are they and where do they come from? Do we really recognize them when they do come to us? I wonder how many are granted in a lifetime. It probably depends more on the breadth of a life than it does the length.

A magical moment, if truly magical is recognized at once. It is quickly and deeply experienced. It is felt throughout the soul. It doesn't stop in the conscious part of our brains or even in the pulse of our inner life.

It is absorbed and assimilated into our very being and it never lets go of our senses. These moments can be brought back to life whenever we call them up, and the thrill is felt anew.

It doesn't have to be a momentous thing as defined by some. But when it comes to you, it is surely magic.

Some adventurous moments I have had would be my standing on the bow of a fishing boat, heading out on the Atlantic, legs braced against the tossing waves, a steaming cup of coffee balanced in my hands.

Again on a boat, on the Pacific, watching a pod of migrating whales breaching and blowing -- coming so close as to be dampened by their spray.

I looked once upon an island, split in two by a dividing line of blue sky and sunshine on one half, black sky and torrential rain on the other.

Gentler magic moments have happened when a butterfly lit briefly upon my nose and looked me in the eye. Swooping sea gulls, coming out of nowhere, deftly snatched bits of my lunch from my hand.

I shall never forget the wonder I felt as I watched my cat give birth. Against warnings that the tomcat would harm the newborns, I saw him softly settle into the birthing box, give a congratulatory kiss to the mother, then go to the task of helping her clean each tiny face.

It is a magical moment for me when a passage in a book fairly leaps off the page and into my heart, as if the author was writing for me only, or possibly about me. It is always thrilling when I come upon a description of a place where I have been and experienced. To experience it again in the written form feels magical to me.

And so I read and study, and travel when I can, seeking those magical moments that always come when least expected.

NIGHT BIRD

It was very dark as I settled in
Ready for sleep.
Suddenly a bird sang outside
My window,
And it felt like morning.

BOOKS

What does the word "book" bring to your mind? You can read a book, write a book, and review a book. You can browse in a bookstore, be a bookbinder, be in someone's book or throw the book at someone.

You could keep the books, make book, or even be booked. A book can have a jacket, a plate, a mark and even have lice!

A book can be in a bookcase, on a bookshelf or a bookrack where there may be a pair of bookends. An avid reader may be called bookish or a bookworm.

To me, books are Treasure, and they make me greedy. I want to hold on to all I have, while longing for more. I very reluctantly lend any, and only to the most trustworthy. I anxiously await their return, like a mother watching for the school bus.

This obsession was not always so intense. While in school, I considered it a great inconvenience to be assigned a book to peruse. What a student I might have been, had I known then, what I came to know later.

My reading journey began in the first grade. "See Spot run, run Spot run." In the teen years and a decade beyond, it was the Romance novels. Boy meets girl, they fall in love, there are problems and they part. Their lives are not worth living, until they meet again, marry, and live happily ever after.

After so many clones with different titles, I discovered the classics of Dickens, the Austens, Twain, Poe, Whitman, and the more modern Hemingway, Morrow-Lindbergh, Kinnan-Rawlings. I should not have attempted to begin such a listing here of all the great and lasting literature … it is infinite.

Non-fiction, biographies, and history soon followed, as my thirst to know about real people and events began to rage. Again, what grades I might have made in history class, if only.

Now we have the Internet with e-books and out of print books made easily accessible. You can even visit the library and utilize its resources through the computer. Well, enough of this meandering. I have a new book to read.

ANTIQUES

It seems to me
That if you are interested
In things antique,
You must be fascinated
with the subject of history.

APPRECIATE LIFE

Think back to what you have done and what you could have done and maybe should have done and didn't. That is your base for what you now are doing and all that you still can and may do.

There is so much to savor and enjoy, despite possible obstacles such as lack of wealth and varying degrees of health. There are limitations of course, there have always been limitations for everyone.

The multimillionaire will die the same as you. So what is great wealth? I like the quip, "Did you ever see a Brink's truck in a funeral procession?" So long as we have breath in our lungs and a beating heart and a reasonable amount of intelligence, we can go on learning and loving and laughing. This is basic.

Too many people curl up in a fetal position and cry for their lost youth and beauty. Turning inward, they miss the excitement of a rapidly changing world. "Things sure are different now" they lament, rather than appreciating that nothing stays the same, nor should it.

With this attitude, they pass right by the ducks and swans swimming in the pond and never see nor hear them. They entirely miss the little child's giggle and the opportunity to smile back. Instead they shuffle out for their morning newspaper and hover over the world's indignities, having never heard the sweet bird's song just outside the door.

So many look but don't see, hear but don't listen, stiffen like stone when hugged and hide their tears of joy. There is a well-known saying, "stop and smell the roses" that really says a lot to us in a few simple words.

Each day is worth noticing and holding close. Fill your days with your own senses and sensibilities and learn as much as you can. Observe, absorb, try new things, share of yourself. Mostly, appreciate life.

IN A SNAP

Impatience put away
The artwork
The camera brought it back

PHOTO COMPOSITION

I've read that "the
greatest joy of nature
is the absence of man."

I would like to add:
So please get out of
My view finder

PHOTOGRAPHING CATS

Oh, what a clever pose.
Wait, I'll get my camera.
Good, they're nicely
Focused and the
Light is right.
Click! Too late,
They're gone.

CAMERA SHY

An animated face
Is funny to behold,
Especially for the
Camera

HORSING AROUND

Wildflowers in a field,
A horse grazing nearby.
Now there's a lovely
Photo.

Close-up of just one
Flower, while
I'm prone upon ground

Light is metered,
Shutter speed set
In focus and ready now;
Too late, the darned horse
Ate it.

LAUGHTER

I like to think of laughter
As the music of the earth
Climbing a giant staff
To thank God for our birth

THAT'S HOW THE COOKIE CRUMBLES

In a flurry of cookie baking every Christmas season I turn my kitchen into a winter wonderland of flour and sugar. I blend in with my environment like the protective-coloration of a brown rabbit in the white snow.

I blame the incessant urge to bake cookies, on the homemaker magazines at the checkout area of the grocery stores. There they are in all their glory, exquisite photos of luscious and perfectly formed, flawlessly decorated cookies.

It's the cutout cookies that really grab my attention, especially when the text reads something like, "you too, can make these easy, perfectly decorated cookies." The word "perfect" is simply not in my dictionary of baking skills.

I diligently follow the directions, reading them over and over again. I chill the dough the required time. I obediently scatter flour over my counter surface and rolling pin, and a few other places not intended. From there I am well on my way to cookie disaster again.

My biggest challenge, and therefore problem, is in the rolling-out of the prepared dough. It loses its chill because I work too slowly and timidly and so it sticks to the rolling pin. The recipe calls for rolling the dough to 1/8th inch thickness. What the heck does 1/8th inch look like and how come I only achieve it in spots? My ready-to-cut dough looks more like a topographical map of hills and valleys, with little torn spots replicating dried-up bodies of water.

I love my collection of cookie cutters. I am especially fond of the trees and stars. In my hands, however, the trees are usually top-less and the stars look more like starfish.

The icing slides off the sides, carrying all those pretty silver beads and colored sugar crystals along with it. I won't even discuss my foibles with the squeezy pastry bag thing.

I don't know why I bother with all this, when most the cookies stick fast to the pan and break into pieces when I try to remove them to a cooling rack. This, of course, makes them fair game for eating on the spot. This is the best part of the whole process.

Even the less adventurous bar and drop cookie recipes are doomed to failure in my kitchen. The drops are more like blobs with no two the same size. It's the same with the bars. This should be simple, but not for me. When I wield a knife, I produce squares and even some triangles.

But despite all this, I do have two things going for me. The first is that the few cookies that make it to keeper-status, do taste much better than they look. The second thing is that I have expert baking friends and neighbors who very generously share their delicious, perfectly formed cookie bounty with me.

ANIMAL LOVER

Ducks make me laugh
Horses make me cry,
And cats do both

BOOKENDS

Identical squirrels
Sit back to back
On twin remnant fronds
Of a palm tree

They are so still
Lest you look close
Enough for
The nose twitches

HIDDEN BEAUTY

The lovely bouquet you sent
Is hidden behind a
Closed door.

A shame, for I love flowers,
But my cats love them more.

SWEET BIRD SOUNDS

I suppose they twitter like this
At other times of day,
But in the quiet of early morning
They are such a
Sweet tweet, uh -- treat
To go with my coffee.

KICKING UP DUST

I envy that little boy over there.
He's swinging from a tree limb,
And his feet are kicking
Up the dust.

That is exactly what I feel
Like doing today.
Is there an age-limit on that?

RIGHT OF WAY

If I could change just one thing
In the world
It would be that the
Golden Rule would be
Strictly adhered to

Thus ending war, and
Your right of way taken
From you on the road

GROCERY SHOPPING

A large portion of our time and a greater portion of our money is spent in pursuit of our daily bread, so we may as well enjoy it. Grocery shopping, that is.

You meet the nicest people in the grocery store, especially in the cat food aisle. There are usually three or four people standing there with furrowed brows, searching through hundreds of varieties of mixed grill, tuna-salmon, turkey and giblets, sliced, diced, mashed chicken this and that.

The conversations are almost always the same. "Will your cat eat that ?... my cat ate it last week, but not anymore ... he really likes this one ... she hates everything ...what do any of them really like?" "Is moist or dry food better?"... Then, a snicker when one lady says, "My cat is getting senile, she keeps sitting in the dishwater."

Choice is making it so that nothing is simple anymore. Everything, not just pet food, comes in several sizes and flavors, colors and scents. Laundry detergent may be powder or liquid, or in little hockey-puck things. It comes with or without bleach and some is meant only for dark colors, or for cold water.

There are tempting varieties of food. That daily bread may be rye, pumpernickel, wheat, potato, multiple-grains, raisin, nut and many, many more. There is even plain, ordinary white.

Remember when real coffee was just coffee, along with decaffeinated, of course. Now there is every kind of roast and blend you can think of, and different ways to grind it, if you choose to grind your own. Or maybe Instant type is your cup of tea (oops). There now are so many flavored coffees that it boggles the mind. Like I said, whatever happened to real coffee?

Oatmeal and corn flakes can still be found, but they are buried behind either extra sugary kids-stuff, or the healthy types that taste like sawdust. Our grocery has two aisles devoted entirely to cereals.

Fruit has always been a problem for me. How do you tell if a cantaloupe is ripe, anyway? It is very difficult to find bananas green enough to not ripen before you get them home. Strange, never seen before fruits, with exotic names keep making their debut in our grocery. Please, I'm having enough trouble.

The aisles are nearly always crowded with people reading labels. How many calories, how many carbs, and is the large a better buy than the economy size?

When you finally do make your way to the checkout area, an hour later than you had planned on, and with your senses reeling, you search for the shortest line. Express does not mean what its implies, and the twenty items or less checkout seems to draw the numerically challenged.

While waiting your turn, there are all sorts of goods near the cash register. There is nothing to do for awhile but wait, so you continue to place impulse items into your basket. Why is it that just when you get into browsing the tabloids, the line speeds up and you have to return it to the rack?

When at last it is your turn, there are still more choices to make, beyond the paper or plastic query of a few years ago, now you must decide on method of payment ... cash, check, credit card, debit card or the store's own card?

I'll say it again nothing is simple. And when you arrive at home, you still have to unload it all and store it away.

Then when the task is finished, you begin your next shopping list with all those things you forgot.

DEFINITION OF DETERMINATION

A cat doing
What you don't
Want it to

COME TO THE PARTY

An old friend arrived
Half hidden behind
Red carnations and a
Flying balloon.

A party all her own

JUST A DREAM

Do you dream
When you sleep,
Or do you sleep,
To dream?

MOTHER V
-- March 28, 1891 - March 25,1980

To me she was a kind of full-blown rose; still sweet and fragrant, but past her days of glory. Still elegant, she was not of this time, more like a remnant of a better, more appreciative time. She had bloomed in a well-tended garden in the late Victorian era. She became my mother-in-law and a cherished friend for nearly ten years.

I was soon to be her son's second wife, when I was invited to her home so we could become acquainted. The questions tormented me; what would she think of me, and whatever will we talk about?

A long time widowed, she lived alone in a small but charming cottage on the edge of a steep riverbank. The antique furniture crowded her diminutive rooms. The largest piece was a full-size grand piano, which monopolized over a third of the living room.

Everything had been moved here from her much larger, grander mansion, further upriver, which had been the family home. It seemed out of place in this modest house, but like her, it was as comfortable as it was adaptable.

In a very short time, I was put at ease. A fascinating clutter of books, magazines, letters, sketches, and knitting was piled high on a marble-topped table before a large window that framed the river view.

Conversation came easily, as we discovered much in common in our passion for reading and our amateur artwork. Though I was from a far more modest background and present means, she never treated me as less than equal to herself.

I knew immediately that I had met a person whom I would soon love, as she softly played the piano, across from a crackling fireplace. Her music was pleasant, lyrical tunes I did not recognize. She read from yellowed, tattered sheet music of another time.

Susan "Sam" LeGree

BIG MACS AT MOTHER'S

We brought take-out
Burgers and fries.

She served on
Limoges and sterling.

YOUR GIFT FROM THE SEA

Why didn't I ask you from where the
Sand dollars came?
Now you are gone, and
They remain.

Why didn't I ask,
When you gave them to me?
Your precious
Treasure.

So delicate and fragile.
Even now they spill their sand
Like the sand of your life
That has all run out.

I would like so much to know
On what beach you walked barefoot
And gathered this bounty that meant
So much to you then,
And now means so much to me.

SUCH A CARD

I can spend an hour in front of the massive racks of greeting cards found so often in so many places. There are cards for nearly every occasion and some for no occasion at all. There are all sizes and shapes. Once I sent my dad a Father's Day card that was so big, it was delivered by UPS.

Cards can be pretty and complimentary, mushily over-stated, or they can simply tickle the funny bone. Some feature photographs, some reprint fine art and others are comical cartoons.

They all have great power and motivation. There have been times when feeling a bit depressed and overwhelmed, I have made it a point to visit the card store. Just reading the cards can elevate my mood.

My fascination with card giving began when the then-called "Contemporary" line was introduced. My friends and I started sending them to each other well beyond the obligatory birthdays and timely holidays. The practice still continues.

We've always favored the snappy one-liners and the insults lurking behind sweet prose. I notice, as we age, we are more often sending cards that express our love and appreciation.

Some cards that one receives are much too difficult to throw away. There are many, which I never have. How can you ever toss away a sweet card from your spouse?

It may be best that I don't tell you about the cards that I receive from my cats on Mother's Day, or about the ones they receive from their cat and dog friends.

But then, you've probably made up your minds about me by now, anyway.

THERE ARE DREAMS
AND THERE ARE DREAMS

One is literal, the other hopeful.
The first disintegrates
The harder you pursue.

The other with relentless
Nurturing
Just might thrive and bloom

43

DREAM TRAVEL

Magic power
Has the dream
That takes me
Back to where
I've been,
And to places
Never seen

KEEP YOUR EYE ON THE BALL

I will never understand it, though I really have tried for years. I'm referring to the intriguing, mysterious game of Football. I suppose the biggest reason I don't understand the concept of this popular sport is simply because I can never - I repeat - never, see the ball! Even in a filmed replay, even when they draw those little white circles on the TV screen. Even when the announcers are explaining in detail, what player has the ball, and what he is doing with it … I seem to always be following a different one.

In all honesty I will have to admit that I have seen the ball a few times, when it was placed on a little disk in the middle of the field and everybody stays away, while one guy runs up and gives it a kick. The camera focuses on it as it sails toward the center of two upright posts in the ground. Then, I lose it. When it is announced that the kick was either good or missed its mark, it is always news to me.

We have been invited to many televised Super Bowl Parties over the years in the homes of friends. I have never failed to have a wonderful time. The food and drink has always been the best and the other guests fun to be with. I always have entered, but never won, the betting "pool" that is designed to make the competition even greater. I don't understand how the "pool" works either.

Actually, I've never seen very much of these televised games, except for the half time entertainment. I also like the commercials. Usually the women group together and talk about all sorts of interesting things, while the men cluster around the television sets, whooping and hollering.

I'm not saying there aren't any women football fans. I have met a few at some of the parties and they really seemed to get into the whole thing. I admire them very much, and the way they point out the ball for me.

Despite everything I've said, I do like football. I love to hear it being broadcast from another room, while I busy myself with the things that I do. I've always thought it has a cozy sound.

I wonder what those big bruisers with the huge shoulders and hard helmets would think of that.

AN AFFAIR WITH MR. COFFEE

He has always been full-bodied, dark and strong, and very warm ... just the way I like him. He has been faithfully waiting for me each morning, ready to please and satisfy soon after I open my eyes. So is it any wonder that I have stayed loyal to him these many years? Indeed, he is first in my thoughts at the beginning of each new day.

I had become so trusting and dependent upon him, that perhaps I became too sure of him and a bit careless in handling him, because one morning as I reached out, I realized something was very wrong.

There was what appeared to be a slight weeping of cool, clear water. Yes, it was true, even though he tried to hide it. Oh, what had I done to Mr. Coffee? I must have somehow hurt him terribly, in my complacence.

I felt awful. He didn't deserve this and what was worse, I would be without him now! In desperation I hurried out to Sears and searched for another just like him.

My aching heart was eased as I saw him in the crowd. He seemed to reach out to me and beg me to take him home. He was a bit more expensive than I had anticipated, but if he were to serve me as my ex-Mr. Coffee had, then price hardly entered into our relationship. And so he came away with me.

We were just becoming comfortable with each other, when I went out for the day and happened on a tempered glass canister at the Goodwill store. It was an exact replica of my former one.

I bought it, brought it home and hid it away. Just in case the new guy ever lets me down.

TIME OUT

Sweet kitty decides to
Curl up on my lap,
And nap.
No problem, that

Except she lays
Across my arms
I cannot reach
The keyboard.

It's time we both take
A break.

TIME RUNNING OUT

I have to accept that
I will never read
All the books,

Nor become a
"Grandma Moses"
nor will it all
be written down.

I'll not have time to
See it all,
Taste and hear it all,

But my soul still
Feels it all

My husband was brutally murdered in a holdup on May 3, 1977
His last words to me before he left that morning, "Be careful today, you're precious to me."

THE PARTY IS OVER

My yesterday was like a party.
People, laughter, fun and love.
The champagne overflowed.

Today a bullet pierced our lives
Yesterday was washed,
And stored in a dark cupboard.

The party has ended,
There's a lock on the door.

1977

JUST FILL-IN FOR MY DAYS

Our marriage was my life
Beyond the day's activities.

What is there now, at day's end?
What use, the day's industry now?

I need no "fill-in" I need a life to live.

A WIDOW'S JOURNEY

I've heard it before, I heard it again today
From the minister, "I'm proud of you."
That's a nice thing to say, I guess.
But I keep wondering why?
They say I'm conducting myself so well.
I'm really "handling it, and
have a realistic and healthy,
Accepting attitude."

I say, what else can I do?

Our friends have been wonderful.
He must be happy if he
Can see it.

Lunches and dinners,
Movies and concerts
Offered to soothe my sorrow.

For several weeks,
I ran and ran
Truly grateful,
But exhausted.

But what now, as the
Invitations are fewer and
Friends go on with
Their lives.

The question, what am I to do?
I somehow fill my days
With the comfort of
Routine, and the mundane

But when the sun goes down
And the telephone no longer rings,
I put aside the awesome lists
Of "must do" concerns.

For which there is no heart

I sit, elbows on my knees,
And stare at nothing.
I stare, and stare,
And still I do not see.
The only sound, a ticking clock

Tonight I finally cried.
Unlike the misty-eyed futility
Of the many months
Now passed.

A gentleman asked me
to dinner, and I
Accepted, surprising
Myself as much as he.

Later, when back home
Alone, it happened,
The wracking sobs
Which overwhelmed.

Susan "Sam" LeGree

Wondering about such
Unleashed emotion,
I realized, --
what I had done, had
forever closed the door
on what had been.
And I mourned anew.

I guess it must be starting now.
The loneliness, or is it boredom?
I've always had a tendency
Toward boredom.

In between it all,
I have little burst of true joy.
For no reason other than
Just being alive.

I suddenly begin to hum
And a hint of bounce
Returns unbidden,
to my step.

Like the sudden clamor
Of a startled bird,
Swooping in flight to
Nowhere in particular

Then it is out of sight,
The bird,
And my happy moment

Should I redecorate the apartment?
Or perhaps buy a home?
We wanted one so.

Maybe I should go somewhere
Should I change my hair?
Buy new clothes?

Would it be good
To paint again, or write?
Should I accept the job
I was offered.
Oh, but that would tie
Me down.

From what?

Remember our dreams;
The things we wanted,
And you worked for?

How happy we planned
To be.
Now, would you believe?
I have those things --
Just me.

They don't make me happy.

It really takes so little
To destroy my independence.
Someone uses "our" words,
Or I find myself, where
We used to go
Together.

Or, I acquire
one of our dreams.
How empty.

It's not the same, without you.

His mother is moving away,
Far away, to his sister.
My dear Mother V

How good for her, but how
I shall miss her.
My friend, and all I have
Of him now

*Time heals all, as we all have been told. And
so it was to be.*

TIME LOST

Where did the summer go?
You are gone and I am here.
It was May
And now, October.

Something must have happened,
In all that time.

LIFE AFTER FIFTY

They laughed and said I was
Now "Over the Hill"
I asked what's bad about that?

It's been a good, hard climb
To the crest of that hill

The views from there
Show adventurous paths
Still to transgress

Albeit downward, it is a
Gentle slope to coast
With so much promise,
on the winds, in my face.

SOULMATE FOUND

The time was right.
He came at life's returning.
I could no longer live each day,
looking back, … yearning
As unpolished stone,
a diamond, in the rough
Kind, honest true love uncut
Facets to my life, … enough!

Chasing sadness from my soul
He awakened a brand new life.
A different one had begun.
In time, I became his wife

MY CHEF

How fortunate he likes to cook
And even to grocery shop.

He loves to do it
And do it with a flourish.

If left to me, we would be,
The two of us, malnourished

LADIES MAN

Tall, dark and handsome, made
The ladies love him
Now not so dark nor handsome, they
Love him still, as he fetches for them
From the high shelves

BLOOMING WHERE PLANTED

An entirely new life was given me in my later years. It has been an on-going gift, which I hope I will live long enough to fully exhaust.

It began when I re-married twenty-five years ago. The marriage brought two male teenagers into my life and home. I have never had children of my own, so this was an experience, that was trying at times, but was not to be missed.

The boys were soon out of the nest and my husband retired at an early age. We made our home in Florida, among others our age and older, and I never looked back. Our community is named "Golden Ponds." It is all that its name suggests.

I don't know to what it might be attributed; my late blooming. In part it was the anonymity it presented, moving to a place so far from all I had known. Always of low self-esteem and confidence, I consciously chose to blunder into endeavors I probably would never have attempted had I not left my hometown.

My husband encouraged me in all I did, and he continues to encourage what I continue to do. He respects my individuality and gives me the space to pursue it. In part, because of this, our love has grown deeper throughout the years.

A LATE BLOOMER TAKES NOTE

I was born nearly a month late, so I was told. Missed out on kindergarten as a result. Too immature for mathematics, I drew pictures and decorated the school's bulletin boards. I learned to regret that.

I was too insecure to know that all I wanted was offered in my school; art, drama, journalism. What would I do in those classes?

I didn't appreciate the classics or history. In my 30's I developed a passion for both. As for passion toward the opposite sex, I was very slow to know what the good qualities in a man should be. I paid dearly for that.

I was 24 when I had my tonsils removed, and 40 before I had my ear lobes pierced. At 50 my teeth were in braces. I sat in the waiting rooms with all the kids.

Age 50 was the year a new life began for me in the south, and this is when I finally opened myself to bloom. Was the soil not rich enough in the north?

I learned to bowl with a team, and sometimes did quite well. I volunteered for many things, from charity to entertainment... and I finally felt I "belonged."

Artwork was pursued for awhile, and I learned to utilize the camera lens. Always finding expression in the written word just for self, I gradually shared it and surprisingly, was paid.

I came to appreciate a good family bond as well as one with God. Blooming late in my small way, is much better than dying on the vine!

SIGHTS AND SOUNDS OF GOLDEN PONDS

This is a peaceful, quiet place. At the same time it is a busy, bustling, full-of-life place. From the soft thump of the morning newspaper delivered to our driveways, until the last "goodnight" is said, the sights and sounds of Golden Ponds are my comfort, my "home sounds."

Many mornings I find my newspaper in the glow of a bright, silvery moon and in the distance sometimes hear a wake-up call from an enthusiastic rooster on the property beyond.

The mocking birds are early riser too, and honor us with their sweet interpretations. Before long the comical crows utter their "uh-uhs" and at any time of day the velvety, ring-neck doves coo their mournful messages.

Most everyone is stirring now. The avid walkers pass by in small groups, announced by their soft chatter. The lone persons are absorbed in the privacy of their headphones.

Bicyclists make their rounds, some headed for the clubhouse. The clubhouse springs to life as the office opens for the day's business. Residents join their friends at the pool or for exercising, card and mahjongg playing, tennis, or any of the many amenities. Tickets are sold and meetings are held as activities are planned.

The mowers and trimmers disturb the quiet only temporarily and that too, is a pleasing sound as they maintain the lush green of our environment. Everywhere you look, are stately palm trees and pines. Many flowering shrubs and other plants display their vibrant color, no matter what time of year.

The rattle of the UPS truck is always welcome, as anticipated packages arrive. The mail person makes the rounds and smilingly delivers to our doors, any mail too large for the mailbox. The not unpleasant sound of refuse and recycling trucks make their appearance on schedule. They are pleasant, accommodating men.

Many cars come and go all through the day, as Golden Ponders go about their daily business, always waving to whomever they pass.

The clubhouses buzz with evening activities, sometimes long after the colorful sunsets reflect on the ponds. Laughter, good-natured teasing and sometimes music travels through the warm, humid night air.

The rows of spherical lamps illuminate the lawns like a glowing string of pearls. Somehow, it is a comforting sight.

My personal vantage point, is the largest pond and looking east. The sunrise competes with the sunset, by presenting its own special beauty. Many times the early clouds are tinted soft shades of pink and gray, which reflect in the still water.

Wading birds come for breakfast, while the ducks and turtles entertain. Rabbits and squirrels take a front row seat, while I at my window, join them as an appreciative audience.

Life is good here.

THE OTHER FLORIDA

Years ago, before I ever dreamed of visiting Florida, let alone living here, I had a preconceived idea of what it would be like.

It would be hot, there would be hot, sandy beaches, with hot nightclubs to frequent, after the hot sun went down. There would be tall palm trees and much taller high-rises in the high rent districts. A fantasy-world, inhabited by Disney characters would be here, as would thousands of tourists from everywhere, united in their own fantasies of Florida.

As I grew older and actually did come to live here, the foregoing description, though accurate, seemed far less predominant to me.

I became interested in reading some of Florida's history and I wandered around a bit, not just looking, but really seeing. One doesn't need to meander very far, west to find a whole different Florida.

There is a massive cattle ranch that in more recent years has opened its gates for pre-scheduled tours. However, before that, I wrangled an invitation and was escorted about by the renowned ranch owner himself. An author and expert wildlife photographer, he was the best guide one could ever hope to have. His love for the land and his life there was apparent with every step.

We set out early in the morning, both with long-range cameras in hand. I marveled at the proximity of wildlife there. Many species, including deer, bobcats, eagles, hawks, and

57

the not so wild Braford cattle herds, developed to withstand Florida's climate and insects.

The cowmen live and work on the spread and look just as I had hoped they would. Tanned, and tall in the saddles of their ranch-bred sorrel horses. Most wore western hats, tilted against the sun, but the occasional rebel sported a baseball cap. All wore boots, as did I, so I wouldn't appear a city slicker.

We feasted on oranges, warm off the trees and pared by the cowman's pocketknife. A magical hammock of ancient live oaks, dripping with Spanish moss, provided its cooling shade. The spreading branches were adorned with brightly blooming bromeliads.

This, the rancher explained, is representative of much of Florida, holding on as best it can.

THE TIME IS RIGHT

All my life it seems, I've had
To put aside
That which I longed
Most to do.
To read, to write, to observe.

Throughout the years, some
Time and effort has been
Given to these things,
But always, daily life
Was in the way.

I am late in my years now
So I set aside all I can,
to indulge my passion.

Am I selfish? I think not

WHERE DID I GO?

Haven't seen you,
People say.
Where have you been?

I've been lost
In the-world-within.

COLOR DISPLAY

This December morning
The rising sun so brightly lit
The bougainvillea,
I thought at first,
It was Christmas lights.

WANNABE STAR

A facet of late-blooming that opened up for me, came as a great shock, when I showed up to volunteer makeup and backstage assistance, for a neighborhood amateur stage production, only to be offered the leading role in the show.

Having never attempted acting, and already nearing fifty, I spluttered that I could not do that, I don't know anything about it, and I'm too old to memorize all those lines! I only came to do the makeup.

I did do it, and went on to the "big time" the lead in a community college production, when they opened auditions for an older woman. What a thrill it was, when I made my entrance the first night, in the first act, and the audience stood and applauded! Flustered, I nearly forgot the opening lines.

I really have to explain here, that the people in the audience, who honored me in this manner, and without my as yet, opening my mouth, were all personal friends and neighbors! The others in the vast auditorium must have wondered who was "this star, whose name they didn't recognize?"

I came back down to earth, and from then on have written and performed comedy for the Golden Ponds community exclusively. More suited to my level of incompetence.

SEEING THE SEA

I am not a beach-person. I don't like suntan oil, bugs nor sand getting into everything. I do not share the enthusiasm of so many who at every opportunity, rush to the ocean's side, throw themselves onto a large towel and expose as much of their skin to the sun as the law allows. I cannot fathom the enjoyment they seem to glean from this sacrificial rite to old Sol, who smiles down on them with unrelenting rays of pure heat.

But, to each his own and different strokes, you know? I do have a secret I will share. Whenever problems or the pressures come crashing down on me, and it all just seems to be too much, I run away to the ocean.

I don't do the "beach thing," I just go there and I look out at all the beautiful color and listen to the surf. I allow the salty breezes to caress my pale skin and tousle my hair. I remind myself anew that I live in Florida. I am not on vacation. I live here. I am privileged to this wonderful therapy whenever I please, and I always come away refreshed.

I doubt that many, whether beach enthusiasts or not, can deny the seduction of the sounds and sights of the ocean. The ever-restless waves that vary in their massive strength, the patterns of the white foam and the little treasures it sometimes presents at our feet. Like a cat or dog begging to play.

The cooled sea air, that allows us to better endure the summer's heat, the funny pelicans awkward on the ground, magnificent in flight. Scampering plovers, and sea gulls in delightful conversation.

There is a hypnotic aura at the ocean's edge that, if only temporarily, lifts up and carries one's worldly anxieties out to sea. On second thought, maybe I am a beach-person after all.

EVERYBODY IN THE POOL!

Like I said, I'm not a beach-person. I'm not a pool-person either, nor do I like showers. For the record, I do take frequent baths; the warm, bubble-scented type where the water is no more than navel-high. I have made a rare appearance at the Golden Ponds pool, from time to time over the years. I think I have dangled a toe in it maybe twice.

Way back, when our granddaughter was but a tadpole, she would beg me to take her to the pool. Like a dolphin, she would swim and play in the water until she was as wrinkled as I am now. She even used to stand on her head in the water. Claustrophobic that I am, it nearly sent me into spasms.

The pool is one of the most popular amenities, probably high on the priority list for many that purchased a home here. Many residents enjoy it daily. Some take part in the pool-exercise program, while others simply "noodle" around.

I made one of my visits not long ago, where I watched the bobbing bodies, topped with colorful head coverings and dark sunglasses. Hardly anyone was recognizable. The men seemed to segregate to the deep end and the women were clustered at the opposite end, happy and playful as sea otters.

Pool side lunches one day each month, are on the activities calendar. This is fine with me, so long as I can sit in the shade, hugging the clubhouse wall. The pool and its surrounding deck are very attractive and bring out the sociability in people.

I could really like the pool, if it wasn't for the sun and all that water!

TIME BRINGS CHANGE

Used to be that I knew everyone in our community, and everyone knew me. We came in just behind the land-movers, and watched it all grow. So many over twenty years have come and gone that it is hard to keep track.

Some dear ones gone forever, others merely moved away. Probably the saddest thing is that some have come and gone, and we never met.

BACK IN MY OWN BACKYARD

Not many people see our backyard. Maybe that is because it is in the back. Across the lawn we enjoy a panoramic view of a large pond and all that goes on there. I never tire of the pallet of colors the rising sun offers; different, one day to the next.

Before the ducks start splashing around, the egrets, herons and cormorants fly in to fish for their breakfast. At times, we see fishers of the human variety, as well.

The backyard, though far from botanical perfection, is host to many good things. There is the ficus tree that now towers over the house and bequeaths its shade, so coveted during the hot summers. It is Sarah's tree, selected for planting by a granddaughter, when both were very small. They are both grown up now.

After much ado, two of three palm trees we planted soon after moving in, have thrived and they wave their fronds in greeting. Beneath them is a small memorial to "Joy" and not far away, others for "Simon" and "Bummer." All are beloved, departed family members of the cat persuasion.

There is Confederate Jasmine which I chose for its name as much as its sweet scent, and there is a double, peach-colored hibiscus that is so enthusiastic, it must be reined in on a regular basis, by the hedge trimmer.

We waited a long time for oranges, but when they finally came, they made up for their tardiness, with abundance. The grapefruit still doesn't know what kind of tree it is.

One year, we feasted on sweet, succulent pineapple, plucked from just outside the back door. Our next door neighbor planted them as a surprise. We often find pretty flowers and plants growing in our backyard, that we did not plant. Everybody should have such a neighbor.

It is said that the grass is always greener on the other side of the fence. Our grass isn't always so very green, and the weeds gleefully take over wherever they can. Weeds particularly like the Florida climate.

I've always been grateful that God, in His wisdom, colored most weeds green to blend better with the grass.

ALL EARS

Maybe it is because I am a boring conversationalist, but I find it hard to hold the attention of some of my fellow retirees. But I have hit on a sure way to stop them from walking away with their eyes glazed over. Just mention an ache or pain, your operation, or whom you doctor is. If that doesn't work, mention food.

MAKING WAVES

Everyone waves
As they pass you on
Our streets.
I think it is the law.

What bothers me, is
Those darkly-tinted
Car windows.

Can't see a person
Inside, but I wave,
Just in case they did

SYMPATHY PAINS

Never complain to a fellow retiree
of life's little health problems,
Like fading eyesight,
Heartburn, leg cramps or
Back aches.
You'll get no sympathy,
Because
They've already been there

WHAT DAY IS IT?

If the neighbors' garbage cans
Are out,
It is either Tuesday,
Or Friday

BYE-BYE SNOWBIRDS

Some people year after year, make the seasonal treks back and forth between their southern and northern homes. In the early fall, some leave with much waving of hands and farewell speeches. Many others simply slip away. You look around one day, and they have flown.

Awnings are fastened tightly over the windows, and the vacated carports stare blankly at the street, newspapers no longer are tossed in the driveways.

Those of us, who make Florida our only home, huddle against our air-conditioners and settle in for the hot, humid, southern summer. The sun beats down steadily and unmercifully and the nearly daily rain showers do nothing to cool the temperature.

When the sun gives up the day and night closes in, dark as the inside of a pocket, (as Mother V would say), the summer concerts begin. I am sorry that the Snowbirds have to miss this fascinating music.

Mother Nature is the maestro of a huge, very diversified orchestra. As the moon rises, the musicians tune up and as the concert progresses, the many varied instruments play their designated parts. Some play in solo, but most in harmony with each other.

The unseen night birds call out from their lofty perches, their lovely songs accompanied by a chorus of throaty frogs, and all-manner of unidentified creatures from the insect world.

Sometimes the night sounds are like the jungle, or what I assume the jungle to sound like. It is eerie, and at the same time, hauntingly beautiful.

In my childhood, during the still of the northern nights, I often heard a distant, wailing of a train's whistle. To me it was the loneliest sound in the world, as I knew it.

The Florida night is some times like that, but instead of melancholy, its music makes me happy.

SNOW DOWN SOUTH

Living in the north,
Snow was not often a
Remarkable thing,
But an expected part
Of the season

Though I must remark,
That the first snowfall of
The year was thrilling

As children we ran and
Played in it and formed
It into playful weapons

As adults we cursed it
As it mired our wheels,
Or worse,
Kept us captive at home.

It strikes me as odd to
Now find myself
Transfixed before the
TV screen.

To watch the
Weather channel and
Shout with delight,
"come, look at the snow!"

LOOK MA, I'M A WRITER

I took a deep breath, entered the newspaper editor's office and blurted out a run-on sentence. "I'm a retiree, I have no formal education in journalism, and I have never been published, but I want to write for you and you don't have to pay me."

He said the price was certainly right, and he looked over the few samples of my written words that I had brought along. I was given the task of writing a monthly column about my community.

The following days were agonizing. "What am I doing, what will I say, how will I ever meet a deadline, who do I think I am?" Since my subject was one so close to my heart, it really was not as difficult as I had feared. I shall never forget the excitement I felt when I first opened the newspaper to see my very own writing and by-line.

Before very long I was hired, (yes, and paid) by a couple local publications and then as a string reporter for a newspaper in a nearby town. I was assigned all sorts of subject matter, and sent out to interview all sorts of interesting people.

A challenge and great fun for quite awhile. Throughout all the years I have remained editor-publisher and columnist for my communities' twenty-page monthly newsletter. It is my great pleasure.

MORE ROOM OUT THAN IN

I must write what spills over
Into my heart and mind
Whether of interest to anyone
Other than myself.

For not to do so,
Burdens and crowds
My soul

DEADLINES

Like spinach and liver,
I don't like them,
But I know they are
Good for me

READING AND WRITING

Everyone who is a reader,
I think,
At some time feels
Compelled to write

DON'T LEAVE HOME WITHOUT IT

Dressed in finery,
ready for the world,
Yet, without pen and paper
A writer is naked

WHAT'S IN A WORD

I love words, but words don't always love me. Sometimes the simplest of them like to escape my mind and cling tenaciously to the very tip of my tongue. Sometimes they don't even get that far! There are times when they pack-up their dictionary and thesaurus and simply leave town.

The spoken word is enough of a problem, but there also is an infliction called "writer's block" which likes to make short visits. The nasty symptoms cause me to become anchored before my computer, stiff fingers poised above the silent keyboard, my glassy eyes staring at the monitor... a very large, and very blank monitor.

This uncomfortable condition usually lasts but a few hours, but sometimes it hangs on like a summer cold. I leave my chair, but the question of "what to write" follows me everywhere. It impudently goes with me to my bed at night and wakes me early in the morning. It chills my coffee and it slips between the pages of my newspaper.

In desperation one day, I turned to the Internet and typed the words, "writer's block." And guess what,... I was advised to write about writer's block!

FISHING FOR WORDS

Hurry, write it down
Pull it in
Before it gets off
The hook

FLYPAPER

Like a pesky fly, the thoughts
Awake me before the dawn.
They flit and buzz
About my mind.

They force me into wakefulness
I can't ignore …
They're so persistent.

And so the coffeepot goes on
And I adhere the thoughts
To paper

PUSHING SIXTY WITH ALL ITS CLUTTER

What a sobering thought, leading to so many more sobering thoughts. I was so ambitious in all that I wanted to say and do and be. I was too busy being young and just too busy being busy, to fully accomplish these many things at the time when the inspiration was there. Those were the things that I would be doing when I was older, had more time, had nothing else to do.

Now, I am there. I am just as busy, maybe more so, but with a vastly different agenda and set of priorities. As I look at the overall picture, I have to accept that there is less time ahead than behind me. I will never get it all done.

The autobiography was always put off, knowing that I still had so much material yet to gather, translated: living to do. With no close family, I wonder if there would be anyone who would care to read it. That would be embarrassing; and after all that work!

I will never be able to read all of the hundreds of books in my library, though I certainly have tried my best. I make it impossible, as I constantly add more.

There also is the matter of photographs to be organized. Not only have I always throughout life, had a camera ready to record every event, I also have fancied myself an amateur "art photographer"... hence the many enlarged images of both wild and domestic animals, including every cat I ever met. The butterflies and gators, the horses and cows, the ducks, pelicans and so many more, line the walls, and spill out of cartons.

I am interested in history, and considered a civil war buff by some, so it follows that I have a great love of travel ... and travel, means photographs.

When younger, the pictures were labeled and placed in labeled albums, chronologically stored. As years went on and the interests grew, and the time to pursue them was mine, I lost the inclination and energy to keep up.

And so, the coveted clutter overflows the shelves and all of my life. But it's all right, because it is cherished and enjoyed.

CLUTTER OF ACTIVITY

I apologized to a visitor
For my very messy desk.

Chuckling, I said, "Clutter is a
Sign of genius."

My friend answered,
"Clutter is a sign of an
active mind."
Her view suits me better

MAKING ROOM

Need room in the
Cupboard?
Break a few glasses

RECIPES MEMORIES

Recently, in the back of a storage closet, I came across a large cardboard box of magazine clippings, index cards and various scraps of paper. Upon closer examination, I realized that I had come upon my life's collection of long abandoned recipes.

I spent a lot of time rummaging through this memorial to long ago dinner parties and entertaining. There were literally hundreds of yellowed, tattered and sometimes food-splattered memories there. The content of the box may not have been a pretty sight to behold, but the archive of delicious, sometimes festive, sometimes challenging culinary successes caused that to be easily over-looked.

My mouth fairly watered as I sat on the floor reading and remembering. It probably says something about me that the greater part of these many recipes, were desserts.

After nearly an hour of this rumination of past repasts, my pulse quickened and the inspiration to actually cook began to overtake my thoughts.

Then I came to my senses and remembered that the whole reason for this entering the storage closet was to get rid of the clutter of all those things I know I will never use again.

I took a deep breath, momentarily closed my eyes, and pitched the whole box into the garbage can.

I have better things to do!

AN OLD PHOTOGRAPH

You brought me a picture of us

Taken years ago.
Not in our youth, but long enough.

Oh, how it takes me back.
Wish it really could

HOLIDAY TRADITIONS

Life changes make it more and more difficult to continue many of the holiday traditions that live on in our memories. But most of us hang on to what we can because well, it just feels right.

The time frame of Halloween through the New Year celebration is rife with nostalgic remembrances back through our years. Human beings seem to require this sort of selective memory. It validates who we are and where we came from. It places us square into the scheme of things.

We don't always have to time-travel back very far, because traditions have a way of beginning with little effort or design on our part. They can be as simple as a Halloween game, a crowded table at Thanksgiving, an exchange of cookie recipes, trimming a community Christmas tree, and embraces at the stroke of midnight.

These things, whether they are carried forward from years past, or are the product of a changing lifestyle, are the things of continuity and comfort. Still though, we are creatures of the moment, we cannot deny precious memories of holidays past. Our senses won't allow such denial.

Halloween Trick or Treating when I was a child, was probably safer than it is today. But I remember dressing up as a hobo or a princess, or a gypsy wearing all my mother's beads, and venturing into the darkness of our neighborhood. Just to be out after dark was scary enough, but it always seemed to turn cold and misty in honor of the occasion. The breezes would blow dry brown leaves around my feet and lurking in the shadows was the imagined threat that the big kids were going to jump out and steal my candy.

The highlight of the evening was always the "must stop" tradition of descending a distant neighbor's basement steps, where cold cider and fresh doughnuts awaited. The only requirement made of the children was to sign their name and age in the yearly log. I never knew the names of these special people, but they knew mine.

The thought of my mother's Thanksgiving dinners still can make my mouth water. She was reared on a farm in southern Ohio, where she learned to prepare basic, filling and fulfilling comfort food. Every Thanksgiving and Christmas I attempt to re-heat the memory meals of my childhood.

Sadly, as we age, the number of family and of old friends dwindles and many of us are far away from those who do remain. Things change, because they have to change.

Holiday traditions are in our hearts, not just our environment. Rather, it is heart that brings them to the environment. When you fill a bowl with treats for the "Trick-or-treaters," the tradition lives one. Whether the Thanksgiving feast is for two or twenty, or if it is celebrated at a church or community group dinner for the needy, the tradition that is Thanksgiving is a living, thriving thing.

Christmas tends to become simpler and more insightful, as we age. Most of us neither need, nor want "things." What we want is the spirit to fill us and overflow in gratitude for the life we've been given on this earth. The spirit is a thing, which we can both give and receive at the same time.

As we go forth from one year to another, our traditions say to celebrate. Champagne and noisemakers and dancing past the magic hour, are wonderful things, but not necessary. Every year, as well as every day, is a gift to be opened by each of us.

How useful that gift is to us, is up to us. We can dwell in the traditions of our past life, or we can instigate new ones. The old traditions will ever live in our hearts.

EVERGREEN

I stood in the middle of a
Christmas tree lot and
Deeply inhaled the scent.

What magic -- I was a child again

EASTER DRESS

I look like
An Easter egg,
All pastels
And oval-shaped

TALKING TURKEY

I like everything about Thanksgiving. Abe Lincoln knew what he was doing when he set the date in the glorious month of November. Living in my tropical Florida home, I have to stretch my imagination a bit and dust off the memories of the northern fields. They were brown with dried corn stalks and baled hay, and the trees were shedding their vibrant cloaks preparing for the crystal ice and ermine snow of winter's fashion.

I decorate with pumpkins, many of them ceramic, and the bittersweet is lamely made of plastic and silk, but our Thanksgiving is as genuine as the roasted turkey.

Thanksgiving meal-memories forever remain prevalent both in my mind and on my hips. Though the number of special people around our table is dwindling, I will ever go all out with a special feast on this day.

It is my deep-seeded belief, that Thanksgiving should be savored and held in high esteem, no matter how humble the repast. It is its uniqueness, which lies in its true meaning, ... a time for giving thanks and being grateful.

AROUND THE TABLE

I have always dreamed of a spacious dining room, with a table that would comfortably seat twenty people or more around it. That was never to be, but it was a nice dream.

When we relocated permanently to Florida, it was to a manufactured home. Such homes do not feature royalty-sized dining rooms. Most people would think it a waste of valuable space, anyway.

Many people when they made this transition, wanted to be rid of their "northern" furniture and start fresh with lighter weight, perhaps wicker and rattan décor in their new tropical homes.

That sounded appealing, but being the sentimentalist that I am, I could not part with my old battered, memory-filled pecan dining room table. It was already fourteen years old when it traveled south with us in 1986.

It sits in all its spent-splendor in the center of our dining space. When it dons its two equally battered extension-leaves, the table overflows into the living room. And though it cannot

75

seat twenty, it does a comfortable job with ten. On occasion a card table has been appended to stretch that to the unlucky seating arrangement of thirteen.

The point of my rambling is ... the old dining room table's scratches and gouges, are easily covered by linens. No one else cares or even thinks about the table, but I am ever cognizant of the friends and family who have graced it.

From the tiny granddaughter smearing the icing of her first birthday cake, to the poignant vision and echoing peals of laughter of those who are no longer on this earth.

How could I or would I ever part with my old dining room table. There are just too many friendly ghosts seated there.

FAVORITE CHAIR

In our house there's a
Pecking order when it
Comes to who sits where.

He has his
And she has hers,
Like papa
And, mama bear

His is large and
Tilts way back
As far as
He will dare

Hers is soft
And swivels round
And rocks away
Her care

LETTER WRITING A LOST ART?

One day it occurred to me that two of my very best friends are "on paper."

My two pen pals have been in my life, one for about 35 years and the other not far behind. Betty is from my hometown, but now lives high on a mountain in North Carolina. She gets lonely sometimes, especially when she's snowed in. But she is a fine artist and spends most of her time in her studio or in her vast library.

I met Carol in the days when I often traveled to New York. She now lives in a renovated Victorian house in New Jersey. She and I share a love of cats, books, art, antiques and writing.

As time slips away and the world changes, changing us as well, we three find comfort and smiles in our frequent letters. We have chronicled the births, deaths, achievements, failures, sorrow and laughter of our lives. It has been quite a journey.

In this time of cell phones and e-mail, it is becoming rare I think, for people to keep in touch the old fashioned way, through letter writing. My friends still write longhand on personal stationery. My penmanship leaves a lot to be desired, so if I can expect to be understood, I type.

It is always a special day when I find a personal letter in my mailbox, mixed in with the bills and junk mail.

DRIVING RIGHT OF WAY

The dreaded day has come, thanks to ever-rising insurance premiums and a fixed income. Our two-car family has become a one-car-two-drivers balancing act. This is no easy thing for two independent people forever on the go, and with poor plan-ahead skills.

Actually, I have to admit that recently my car has stood in the driveway gathering dust and spiders for a week at a time. I can ground myself for several days at a time, writing and pursuing the less productive things I do on my computer. When not on the computer, I might be found "fighting the civil war" through my books, or organizing stuff. Organizing can take a lot of time, but worse is the time I spend trying to find what I efficiently filed away.

So, we are adapting quite nicely to the car scheduling. I like to take one day per week to go treasure hunting for my so-called antiques. My husband has the car on Mondays. That is his etched-in-stone, golf day. One does not mess with golf day. In fact, it is so sacred that I have signed an agreement to not expire on a Monday.

Other than those two days, we don't fight much. The real challenge in our sharing a car is a physical one. When one driver is six foot five, and the other is five foot four, a lot of adjusting has to be made. As you might expect, there are no quick getaways.

When I enter the car after my husband has last driven, the steering wheels hits me in the knees. A lever quickly raises it, but then I cannot reach either gas nor brake. There is a set of clever electric buttons that bring the seat forward and upward. Then, I must bring the seat back from its near reclining mode, to snug up against my back.

Nearly ready to back out, I realize that the rearview mirror is showing me a great view of the car's ceiling. After much fiddling with that, I am on my way, but wait … I can't see anything out of the side mirrors. Not anything that would be the least bit helpful when I'm traveling the inter-state, sandwiched between monstrous semi-trucks.

Another smart little button makes that adjustment, just as a full blast of frigid, maximum fan air-conditioning freezes my sinuses, giving me an instant headache. Once I have returned the settings to low-fan, normal air, and the category six roar has stopped, there is one final, change to make.

We each have a radio station programmed. His is political talk, talk, talk! Mine is soothing golden-oldie music.

On my way at last. As I reach the first stop sign on our corner, I try to remember where I am going.

WHAT DAY IS IT?

Did I bring in the mail,
Or was that yesterday?

Oh, I guess I didn't --
And it wasn't,
Today is Sunday

GIMME A BREAK - 2001

Never thought of church as a dangerous place, but that is where I broke an ankle. All I did was turn to the person behind me to offer "peace be with you." Seems innocent enough to me!

I hesitate to write about this, but frankly, it was all that was going on in my life for about six weeks. I had a lot of time to think about physical handicaps while my leg was entombed in a plaster cast from mid-foot to the knee.

Anyone with a handicap of any magnitude is certainly viewed by me in a completely new light now. While I have always felt regret for anyone's incapacity, I never fully realized how frustrating and magnified, the "little" things can be.

Example: Anything you want is always in another room. I started out on crutches and nearly broke my other leg. Then a friend gave me a walker to use. Five legs are far superior to three.

Maneuvering around, leaning on a walker is very hard on the hands, so I soon became an efficiency expert and learned to multi-task. When I need to make the dreaded journey to the bathroom, which gets further down the hall each time, I mentally make a list of all that I can accomplish along the way.

I begin by swinging my swivel chair around, and with fingertips, push my empty coffee cup to teeter on the edge of the kitchen counter. (a small house can be a good thing). I then pull myself up on my good leg, and grab my life-line walker. The newspaper is tucked under my arm to be dropped onto the recycle pile. I place yesterday's stack of mail into my plastic "designer" Wal-Mart bag (which is tied to the walker's support bars), to carry along until the next time I am able to reach the checkbook and pay the bills. Then I turn off all the lights along the way that have been left burning far too long. I place my daily dosage of pills into my duster pocket so I'll have them handy when time to consume ... stoop to pick up pills off the floor, that fell out of my pocket yesterday, and my mission is completed.

Now I am ready to hop to my computer chair, where I sit on the poor cat, which squeals and give me a very nasty feline scowl

Sweating and panting, I long to turn the air-conditioner setting lower, but the dang thermostat is way down the hall, where I just made my sojourn. My heart finally settles down to a rhythmic beat and my body temperature returns to normal.

Now there is nothing to do but play with the computer and read until my eyes glaze over. I am very fortunate to have a husband who cooks and takes care of me. But oh, I am crawling the walls! That is no easy thing with a leg in a cast.

SAY WHAT?

Many different kinds of ducks enjoy the pond in front of our church entrance. It had been raining all during the services one Sunday morning, and as everyone scurried to their cars, most everyone had an umbrella.

I remarked to a woman walking next to me, that there certainly were a lot of different colored ducks. She responded, "Yes, there's a plaid one, a striped one up there, and over there is a green and yellow polka dot." I smiled to myself as I realized she must have thought I was commenting on the umbrellas!

DON'T SAY IT IF YOU DON'T MEAN IT

Please don't wish me
A nice day, when
The words have little meaning

I cringe at,
"Have a good one" and
wonder, a good what?

The absent-minded mouthing
Of clerks, waiters and such
Rings hollow, as I smile
And say, "You too."
And find they do not
Hear me

ROCK OF AGING

Side by side in our
Rocking chairs
We promised to
Be, when old

Alone on my porch
Just one chair
Don't wait anymore
I've been told --

He's off his rocker

SEEING IS BELIEVING

What's wrong with the windshield that I can't get it clean enough. And, have you noticed that all the road signs need painting? Even the blue carpeting in the bedroom was beginning to gray.

Wiping my eyeglasses for the third time in an hour, I decided it must be time for new ones. The results of a full eye examination proved it was my own eye lenses that were smudged.

For a moment I thought my hearing was going too, when I heard I was getting two Cadillacs. Wow, said I, one would do just fine! Of course the word was cataracts and I was shown into a small room to view a video on the subject, to prepare me for what was to happen next.

In our community, I've learned to never think I have a big announcement to make, if it is about a routine medical procedure. Whoever you tell the news, has already been there, tells you it was a breeze, and changes the subject.

I must admit they were right. The cataract removal, one first and the second one a week later, was not too bad at all.

I now can see for miles without glasses and the world has brightened considerably. Problem is, I can't see my hand in front of my face. So I got a pair of teeny, granny glasses for reading. Very fashionable.

Driving and reading problems were solved. The computer is another challenge. Wearing reading glasses, I must tilt my chin down to see what I have just typed, or to read my e-mail messages. Then, I must tilt my head backward to see the keyboard or to copy any written text. The eyes are good, but my neck is killing me.

TO "E" OR NOT TO "E"

I wonder if all those vitamins
And minerals I swallow
Are doing anything positive

I feel pretty good
But maybe I still would
If I spent the money
On something more fun

Articles abound on what's good
For this and that
It seems as soon as you're
Convinced, they refute
What was said before.

Worse, is that very soon
The whole thing changes back
Who knows?
Guess I'll continue my philosophy
"Can't hurt, might help"

OFFICE CALL

Time for a check-up so I go
See the Doc.
Any complaints? No,
I feel fine.
That's good to hear
Ninety-five dollars, please.

FADING LOOKS

Mirror, mirror
On the wall
I won't ask
If you won't tell

IF THE SHOE FITS

When I was six months from Medicare and living the good life in Florida, I began to realize that the changes in my life were going to be more than I had anticipated. One of the most dramatic, was when I began to accept the fact that I was going to have to weed out some shoes.

The shoe-thing is something most men don't understand and never will. I mean, they actually buy shoes when their old pair wears out! However, my sisters out there understand perfectly.

A girl can never have too many shoes. Another thing men can't understand, is if one finds a simply gorgeous pair of shoes, the only pair left, and they are substantially marked-down, we may buy them even if they are a half size too small.

Shoes don't have to be comfortable, so long as they match the outfit and you don't plan to do much walking. These are set aside for the theater or a dinner in a nice restaurant. One that does not have a dance floor.

The reason for the attack on my shoe closet was prompted in part, by the tropical climate in which I now make my home.

The first to go were my butter-soft Italian leather, knee-high, faun colored boots with the three-inch stacked, heels. I was heartbroken!

But, carrying on with determination, my riding boots and four pairs of western boots were next. Gone, along with my equestrian dreams. One pair of snow boots however, has been pushed to the back of the closet, in the event I ever have the need to return to Ohio in the winter. You have to be practical about some things.

The other reason for this ruthless abandonment, was that nasty three-letter word, age. Not the shoes age, though some have been with me a very long time, but mine.

The time had arrived when I needed to make room for flats and the (shudder) walking-shoes. Everyone knows that high-heels make you appear taller and slimmer. I haven't really gained weight, I've just had to give up my high heels!

All those lovely colors and fabrics and styles. Where would I wear them now, if I could wear them? I gazed at them lovingly as I brushed away the dust. The soles aren't even soiled on some of them.

Would that I could say the same for my soul.

9 TO 5

The work day?
It was for many years
Now, it is my
Coffee formula

INSTANT GRATIFICATION

I like instant stuff
Like silk flowers
And photos from
A digital

But don't serve me
Instant coffee
That must be lovingly
Brewed and bubbled

CURVES

As a girl I had natural curves
I had no need to think about.
Now I go to a place called
"Curves"
Where to have them, I must
Work-out

BROADENING

Sitting while I write
Broadens my mind

Really have to exercise,
That's the "bottom" line

WHAT ?

Hastily scribbled notes to myself
That I cannot read
What does it say? Did a good
Thought get away?

PANIC

Sunday morning,
The paper is late!
Call 'em, call 'em

PACKING IS AGE-RELATED

Been doing a bit of traveling and traveling means packing. I love to travel, and I hate to pack.

While packing I have to think too much about things I would rather not think about, like will it rain? Will it be hot? Cold? Will this "go" with that? Do these shoes hurt?

I remember when I was young, I would throw in a couple mix and match tops with what was then called slacks (pants were the undies). There would be a pair of flat shoes and a pair of slinky high heels, something sparkly for evening, and a nightie for later evening.

Of course, that was just the clothing part of packing. As for cosmetics, etc. there was a toothbrush and paste, a compact and lipstick and some aspirin in case I stayed too long at the party.

How the suitcase contents have changed. There are no high heels and certainly nothing remotely sparkly.

There are a great deal more cosmetics that do far less for me. A must have, is my super magnifying mirror, so that I can see whatever it is that I am trying to beautify. There's tweezers and clippers, scissors and nail file … ready for a fight with airport security.

There is a hair dryer, hair spray and a curling iron. The bag is getting heavier. The usual toiletries go in, of course, but then I can't decide on just one cologne. So there are at least two; and oh yes, nail polish in case I get a chip.

Now, a big plastic box, partitioned into days of the week, that holds the life-sustaining vitamins and prescription meds. There is a multiple and an extra C and E, in case the multiple might now be enough. The calcium horse-choker is next to the low dosage aspirin, to be sure the heart pumps through the night. The cholesterol pill is important, so that I may go on eating the wrong stuff.

Now comes the mouthwash, deodorant, cough drops, band-aides, eye drops, Alka-seltzer, Tums, Chapstick, hand lotion, lots of Tylenol, and oh, must never forget the Imodium!

Wonder what I've forgotten. Oh well, I think I'll just stay home.

NOT IN MY MIND

My family is gone now
My friends are getting old
Why am I the only one
Who has kept old age
On hold.

I don't change, I'm just
The same
As ever, deep inside
Still the girl I always was
Within,
Where the spark
Resides

SECOND OPINION

I feel good,
Except for when I don't.
Mostly small things,
You know
Like pains that
Come and go.
They sometimes slow
Me down

Wonder why I get tired
Some times
Or my knee hurts
On the stairs
Doctor answers
You're getting older.
I softly mutter,
Oh

I HATE SPRING

Spring is the time of year
When I am squeezed, by
Taxes and the annual
mammogram

SMALL TOWN SURPRISE

Quite often I write about what I call the "real Florida, and the old South." Not long ago, we drove through northern-west Florida to destination Alabama and Georgia, and their civil war sites.

The old Marquis suddenly began to shiver and shake. Suspecting it was tire trouble, we pulled into an old gas station on west I-10, shortly before our planned northern turn on Rt. 19. We were told there was a "man out back" that would change a tire, but if we felt we could make it a few more miles to Monticello, we could find a tire dealer there, across from the city hall, who would take care of our problem for less money. Being given that information was pleasant surprise, number one.

Since we couldn't see any damage to the tire (we were not even certain which one was the culprit) and since none of them were going flat as yet, we bounced along. Before very long, we rounded a curve and up ahead loomed the ivory white City Hall building, looking every bit like a giant wedding cake. We were in Montecello, Florida, near the Georgia border.

As I gazed around, it seemed to me that we had driven back in time. The square was lined with live oak trees, dripping Spanish moss. Deep pink crepe myrtle bloomed in profusion. It was so quiet, you could hear the bees going about their business.

Lovely old matronly homes were all around. They were columned and shuttered, and hugged by sprawling gingerbread verandas. On several, there were wicker chairs and porch-swings, well utilized by curled-up cats, oblivious to the world.

As two clean-cut young men attacked the tire problem, I went into the small office in search of a cold cola. Two doors stood open to the oppressive July heat. An elderly gentleman rose slightly from a cane chair and sat again, briefly touching the brim of his straw hat. He softly offered a "How-do, Ma'am." After removing the soda from the cooler, I was about to pay the Southern gentleman, when I realized he too, was a customer waiting for his car repair.

I placed the money next to the unattended cash register that stood but a few feet from the open door and wondered … could this really be the year 2000?

GOING AWAY

Wild anticipation,
A gentle pulling-back
Mixed with, "Let's go!"

Seems a trip is over
In the blink of an eye,
And I'm back
In my chair

THE NATURAL BRIDGE - 2002

My favorite season of the year is practically imperceptible in Florida except for an occasional drop in the humidity level. So I was delighted to be dwelling in the midst of Autumn as I remember it, when I attended an Elderhostel based at the Natural Bridge.

Just south of Lexington, Virginia at the southern end of the Shenandoah Valley the sights and scents of fall wrapped me in a colorful embrace. The natives said the leaf color was not at its best, due to a long-standing draught in the area, but the display was glorious in my eyes.

I struggled down the 125 steps deep into the gorge that formed the Natural Bridge ages ago, knowing full well that the trudge back up again would be much more of a challenge.

Once deep into the depths, I was transported to the cool, crispy memories of the autumn seasons of my youth. The rusts, golds, reds and yellows of the leaves were set off by the deep green of the pines. Some leaves rained down upon us and crunched underfoot.

How I love that sound and so I dragged my feet through them and picked up hands full of them to toss into the air. I caused a few raised eyebrows; but those people probably hadn't gone "fall-less" nearly so long as I had.

The narrow path sloped ever downward, past 1600 year old partial-cadavers of Arbor Vitae trees, then leveled off when the "bridge" was in sight. Muscovy ducks splashed in the trickle of water that still remained from Lace Falls. Above the ducks, on the side of the steep rocks, as legend has it, were the initials of George Washington who long ago surveyed the area. Thomas Jefferson later purchased the natural bridge and the land around it. I was in great company.

As I continued beneath the arch and beyond, the pleasant aroma of burning logs and leaves filled the air, and threads of smoke curled upward. There was a small Monacan Indian Village, still in reconstruction. The Indians were showing off their skills. Deer meat sizzled on a flat rock over a small fire. Dried corn and gourds were a feast to the eyes and the memories of fall.

Retracing my steps, I suddenly became aware of how cool the air was and this Floridian delighted in the simple fact that she had a very cold nose!

FREEDOM

I used to worry because the house
Was not tidy,
My every hair not in place
It's great to be free from all that
I kind of think I'd like to be
Known as an eccentric

TUNING IN

My dreams are so
Entertaining,
I cannot wait to
Go to bed

Always in vivid color,
The volume set just right
Never a commercial
And I am the star

POOF!

Like night dreams
Thoughts run through my mind
But are often gone
Before the telling on paper

BACKSTAGE

Another variety show was conceived and delivered at Golden Ponds after the labor pains of many rehearsal hours. I don't know how the others feel, but each time I am asked to take part in "the show" I shudder, my mind empties, my legs turn to jelly and my backbone becomes a bright yellow. "What can I do? I have no ideas, I have no talent, I have little time and less energy, ... OK, when do we start?"

I was asked what goes on backstage during the performances, besides the costumes, that is.

As might be imagined, there is a lot of anticipation mixed with the hair spray and makeup applications. A lot of people in a small area vie for a tiny space to make their various changes of clothes, shoes and props, all the while hoping to hang on to their modesty.

If there were a tape recorder going, the playback would consist of a muffled jumble of "where's my hat? Anybody got a safety pin? A hair pin? Where are my tap shoes, I left them right here. Will you zip me please? My eyelash just fell off! Will you unzip me please? How's my hair look? You've got my shirt on, where is yours? Wow, look at all the boa feathers, it looks like there's been a chicken fight here. I think I'm gonna be sick. How do you girls wear these high-heels? (That one from a guy) How do my bosoms look?" (Also from a guy.)

Then, the house lights dim, the curtain opens and the sweet sound of applause runs through the veins like life-giving blood. The first guffaw of audience laughter catches the stomach butterflies in a shimmering net and flings them into the mesmerizing spotlight.

Those behind the scenes listen as intently to their fellow-performers as if each line was being heard for the first time, and we smile and applaud along with the audience. I guess that is why we do it.

VANITY

With great hope, I purchased
An expensive eye-bag cream

Should have bought
A hand bag

CATS I HAVE LOVED
(A MUCH-CONDENSED VERSION)

I feel certain that it all began when I was very young and my grandmother, Daisy came to live with us. She was allowed to bring along just two of her many little friends. The lucky two were a yellow-orange tiger named Puddy and a large, gray extra-toed male called Jumbo.

When the time came for me to leave the nest for one of my own, I felt a strong longing for a cat companion. From the first one that came to live with me until my final years, I was ever cognizant that my life was never complete without a cat.

The first, as most of them to follow, was adopted from the Humane Society. She was a little bundle of long gray fur that

I named Misty. The popular song, Misty, was my favorite at that time.

She was so small, that she cuddled inside the opening of a tissue box for her naps. My cats, for safety sake, would all be kept inside at all times. I cherish a memory though, of one breezy fall day when I took Misty out in the yard and watched her chase the swirling leaves.

Misty grew up. One day she began to writhe and roll around the room, uttering the strangest sounds I had ever heard from an animal. Child-woman that I was, I made a panic call to the veterinarian and described my cat's actions. I learned, in his words that Misty was in "season." I would need to have her spayed.

I had a roommate who was not as diligent as I was in making sure Misty did not get outside. Before I was able to get the cat in for her surgery, she became "with kitten." This was one reason why I moved on to another apartment by myself, except for Misty, and company of course.

As the time was drawing near, I assembled a very cozy birthing bed for the mother-to-be, in a shallow box filled with fluffy towels, just inside an open closet. She showed a great deal of interest in it.

One day after work, I climbed the stairs and there was no pet to meet me. I dashed to the box in the closet and it was not occupied. Then I noticed a lump in the middle of my bed, under my snowy-white bedspread. I pulled the cover back and there was mother cat with one kitten still attached by the umbilical cord. I scooped my right hand under Misty and my left under the baby, and placed them in the birthing box. There were no siblings.

In time, things became unsettled and I found another home for the two, as well as another home for myself. My next feline friend was a lovely, calico that I named, "Martini." I don't know why I chose that name, as I never drank martinis. She and I went through a number of moves together, ending in a wonderful carriage house, which stood behind the main house of my landlords. A large window overlooked the driveway where I was told Martini always appeared when it neared the time for me to return from working. I never saw her there. I think she jumped down as soon as she saw me, so as not to appear too anxious.

I remember painting a life size picture of Martini's face. After its completion, I held it near the floor so she could look at it. She arched her back and her fur stood on end. There was a loud hiss and she scampered out of the room. Everybody's a critic!

My first Siamese was an ever-undersized blue-eyed Sealpoint. He was a gift from my soon to be husband, and I named him Happy. We all moved into a pretty town house and life was good. Warm weather weekends were spent on our boat where Happy prowled the decks, attached to me by a nylon cord. This was a necessary precaution I felt, because little Happy was accident-prone.

He liked to eat things that were not edible. After just two years, he was poisoned by the preservative treatment that was on our Christmas tree. The last real tree I would ever have.

We purchased another Siamese from a breeder who at the time had no kittens to sell. Because I was so distraught, she reluctantly let us have the six month old, if we assured her we would lend the cat to her for breeding, when she was ready. When that time came, I called the woman and was told she now had another female and to forget the agreement. The pretty cat was named "Joy" in honor of Happy, and because she brought joy back to me.

Then, one day along came, "Bill." He was a scrawny and dirty Siamese, wearing a collar, but looking as if he had been on the loose for a long time. Despite his deep-azure eyes, he was not a pretty sight.

The only thing to do, after we had no success in finding his owner, was to nurse him back to health and spread our love a little further. Bill responded quickly. His thin body filled out and his coat became glossy. Apparently Joy found him very attractive, because without our knowing when it happened, she was a mother-to-be.

This turned out to be a joyous time for all of us. Joy's belly grew rounder and the movement within rippled her sides. Again I prepared a birthing box and this kitty used it. I found her one day; with one kitten still attached, just as it had been with Misty. As I sat on the floor and rubbed her head, Bill and I watched each of the six kittens come into the world. The last and largest, was stillborn.

It amazed me to watch Joy's mothering. She seemed to know exactly what to do as she cleaned each baby and nestled it close to her body to nurse. Bill was very interested in the whole procedure.

I had heard horror stories about the male cat killing their young and so, I kept Bill away from his family. One day, however, he slipped in. I found him snuggled in the nest with mother and babies. He was washing each tiny face, as well as that of mama Joy.

Another special cat was named Simon, a Maine Coon cat. She was beautiful, loving, and sensitive to our emotions. One last Siamese made the trip south with us. Bummer was a character of renown. Simon, Joy and Bummer rest in our Florida back yard with little markers. Each lived for eighteen years.

BUMMER THE SIAMESE

After more than eighteen years,
My joy and delight,
My sometimes irritating,
Always fascinating
Blue-eyed, purring friend
Has given all his
Time to me

ANNIVERSARY PARTY

I cleaned the house
I mean, really cleaned.
It began around Christmas
And ended on March 5 th
Our twenty-fifth anniversary.

I don't know why I did all that.
In another twenty-five years,
I'll just have to do it
All again.

TO DO LIST

Much to be done
Like cleaning house
Exercise, and
Time with spouse

Day in day out,
It's all the same,
Think I'll just play
A computer game

YOUNG NEIGHBOR GONE

I constantly ignore the knowledge
That there is no
Constancy in this life.

Will I ever learn that
The "Mikes" of this world
Will not forever greet us
With a smile?

SOCIAL LONER

How can it be as one?
An enigma
Oh, how I bloom and beam
When socializing

Yet how I hurry back to
Retreat into silence
And introspect.
Two separate people

KATE

Always, after spending
Time with you
I smiled all the
Way home

I had a friend named Kate. The years of our friendship are my most prized possession, and her death, my greatest loss.

In later years it has been harder for me to become close friends with other women. I have many, many acquaintances of whom, I am very fond. But the attention and devotion that is required for close friendship, now is harder to come by, much as I long for it at times.

Kate softly and sweetly thrust herself through my barriers, and without resistance I opened up my life, my heart and my mind to her. She was a rare individual, selfless, affectionate, funny, warm and caring. She listened to others so intently that she made them feel as if they were the most fascinating persons on earth. That is the way she always was with me, and at the time of her death, many others said the same.

We were best friends, not of any group of friends, but we were as close as any two individual women could be. She was thirteen years older than me, but was far more active and energetic. Kate was young for her years, in appearance, attitude, and enthusiasm.

We traveled together when we could, and we shopped, lunched and enjoyed many things. Best of all, were our heartfelt conversations. We talked of what was current and what had past; our lives, loves, heartaches and the hilarity of it all.

The retrospection we confided, along with the bottomless laughter, was a therapeutic gift, each from the other. I was blessed to have such a friendship and know it will never come again.

We spent her last day together; she went suddenly in the night. I find consolation in the words passed on to me, "Don't cry because it is over, smile because it happened."

Still, I will miss her forever.

IMPROVING WITH AGE

I don't worry the way I used to
Is this because of age?
Maybe not so much time left
For the things I worry about,
To ever happen
That's one consolation of
Getting old

FORMAL TEA MOCKERY

Just for fun, we gathered
And played "Ladies"
Amber colored tea was
Offered from brightly
Polished silver and
Received in delicate
China cups.

Cubes of sugar nestled within
Crystal bowls, resting on
White linen cloths

The scent of flowers and
Soft chords of stringed
Instruments floated
On the air

Hatted-heads bowed to
Savor cloned-scones, and
Other delicacies

A scene from a more
Genteel time, made
Modern by the question,
"Does one remove the
gloves while eating?"

FALLING

As children, playing
Hard, we often fell
And bounced back up

Mom kissed our scrapes
And dried the tears
And off we went again

Now to fall,
Is a greater fear
The years have made
It so
We aren't as apt to
Bounce, but to break!

CHARGING BATTERIES

I have a plug-in charger
That re-charges batteries
For my digital camera

In less than an hour
They are good as new
Wish it would work on me

PAJAMA PARTY

Early morning,
From separate homes
Three women in robes
Emerge as one to
Retrieve the morning news

WERE YOU THERE ALL THE TIME?

Though I saw you often dad, the time we spent was so contrived, turning to rote. Visitation it was called, and as one enters the home of a near stranger, it was uncomfortable, even with the hospitality given.

You no longer spoke to me as a father, but rather as a weekend host. You didn't play the banjo for me, nor ask about my grades. The woman, not my mother was ever present. Trying to befriend, she never realized how much I wished to spend a part of the time, with only you.

And so, we were never again as we were in my earliest years. I grew up, as all children must, and went about my search. For many things, and for you.

At last, I thought I found you in the one I came to love, but much too soon, he met his tragic fate. I turned to you dad, and you came. I rushed to you and found only stiffened arms at your sides. But you took me home.

You stood next to me through all that had to be done, and you offered your help. You held my arm, when I nearly faltered.

It was then that I came to know that it must be me, to say it first. I love you. You hardly knew how to react, until after repetition, through the days, you finally said it back.

With time you said it first, and you reached for me each time I entered or left your home. You were old now and your arms though still stiffened, (from age and hard work), enfolded me.

103

SMELLING GOOD FOR HEAVEN

Every morning as I start my day
I spray on some cologne
Even knowing that on that day
I'll just be home alone.

I have so much of it,
I've noticed with a sigh
Better use it up real fast
Before the day I die.

PLAY TIME

The other world of
My concentration
Is interrupted by a soft
Mew and a well-placed
And much beloved
Rubber band dropped
Daintily, at my feet.

Kitty begs me to throw it
For her to fetch, and
Reminds me, she is still here.

DAISY AND KATIE

We could not remain cat-less for long, and so a trip to the Humane Society was made in early 2003. We were singled-out by two pair of amber-green eyes. They followed our every move, and drew us to them, knowing full well, we could not resist.

The tiny tabby sisters had silver stripes over black, still deciding upon their pattern. My eyes slid back and forth between them, trying to see some identifying marks, one from the other. They each wore a different color collar so the staff could tell them apart.

Beyond the collars, I noticed a slight difference in their face-markings. One had a dimple-like spot on each side of her face. The other had a spot on her left cheek, but stripes on the right.

There was no breaking-up a set, we felt, so the girls both came home with us, and have been delighting us ever since. I named them Daisy (my grandmother) and Katie (my good friend).

Everyone who sees them, asks how we can tell them apart. It has become an easy thing because they are so different. Either one, if we had not taken the pair, would have fulfilled our description of a perfect pet.

One will lounge with crossed forepaws, while the other sprawls. One flattens herself on her back on the floor, while the other prefers the back of a chair, with her legs dangling.

Daisy stays close to me while I am at the computer. Sometimes, too close, as she perches atop the monitor and stretches her feet out to me. Sometimes, she will lie upon my lap with her loud purr resounding.

Katie shuns the lap, but plays endless games of fetch the rubber band between my husband and me. She rarely purrs, but she does kiss!

They hold a daily wrestling match that never becomes unfriendly. They have their cuddle times together, but are just as happy apart.

Daisy is a clown, Katie an imp. Like twins, they like to deceive and sometimes play each other's roles. They both chastise us when we sneeze.

Daisy holds up her paw for a "high-five" when I pass her chair. Katie has a slight preference for "her dad" and actually will sit upon his lap for short periods, but never on mine.

I usually retire first, and it is never long before they both join me. They make their bed on a pillow just above my own. As they have grown, my position in the bed, has become lower and lower, so that my toes are now exposed.

I am an early riser, but if Daisy thinks it is time, she nibbles those exposed toes. A new day of feline-fun has begun.

NO TRESPASSING

Two sister cats, lying side by side
Gaze tranquilly out the window.
Suddenly their tails swish
In unison and
They chatter a duet.

A squirrel or bird has come
Into view.
What nerve, to invade
Their territory!

AMARYLLIS

A flash of bright red
Catches my eye
The amaryllis
Is in bloom!

Planted around the
Side of the house,
I would not know,
If it didn't peek
Around the corner

To tell me it, and
Spring, are here.

WHO?

You know, that woman that
Married that guy --
Oh yeah, used to live
Somewhere.
Uh-uh, and worked at
That place.
I know who she is,
Just can't place her face.

FIFTY YEARS FRIENDS

Can it be, it's been
that long?
What's happened
To those girls

Tears and laughter
Lived as one

What next?   And
Where's the fun?

TROUBLE IN PARADISE - 2004

It was said by many that our area was overdue.   In the twenty-plus years that we had been here, and for many years before, the winds had flirted all around us but never came near enough to cause real damage.

And so, five hurricanes in one season made their Florida visits. Two nasty sisters named Frances and Jeanne, actually moved in with us. At the urging of the Sheriff's Department, we carried Katie and Daisy to our car and evacuated north, leaving the storms to do their will.

Nearly a year later the hurricanes continue to intrude on most every social gathering, and the description given by those who stayed to face them, still causes me to shudder. I will ever be thankful that we sped away from their path, although being away brought the nearly unbearable anxiety of not knowing.

Will we have a home? What is happening back there? Who stayed in the area, and are they safe? How is our beloved Golden Ponds faring? Out of communication for days, no way to get answers, finally there was access to a computer. Bits of news were garnered, for which we were grateful, but mostly the news would only spawn more questions.

Back home at last, without lights or anything electric, the summer heat was oppressive. We thanked God constantly for our personal good fortune and for the fact that no one was injured.

Homes were destroyed in total or in part, the roads were impassable with fallen trees, aluminum and other debris. Our friends and neighbors, returning every hour, wandered around gazing with unbelieving eyes at what had been our lush and tidy community.

Assistance arrived, and provided precious ice and water, and later some food. We warmed coffee and cans of beans on our propane grill, and dined by candlelight, while fighting off the mosquitoes.

Neighbors reached out to each other, willing to share whatever they had, if it was only a shoulder to lean on. For a long period of time, despite the smiles and community spirit, a deep sadness seemed to hang on the air.

As our own immediate needs were met, we ventured out to view our town and its beaches. Everywhere, familiar places were nearly unrecognizable some completely gone, some damaged beyond repair. Others, for reasons only Frances and Jeanne might explain, were unscathed.

As I write this, it is nearing time for the 2005 hurricane season. There are many blue-tarp covered roofs and some homes have only just had their claims settled and contracted workmen. The wait has been long for many, due to so much demand and not enough workforce and materials. But it improves each day. The slight damage at our home has been repaired and we hope for the good of us all, as the season nears.

A lone roof shingle still dangles in the branches of a tree next to our driveway. I leave it there, so I'll not forget to thank God each day.

SARAH'S TREE

The big brave ficus
Is leafing once again.

It only has one
Arm now, that reaches
toward Heaven

The other was blown upon
The house
And was taken away.

What is left, is
Still hugged by the
Strangler fig
That joined it years ago.

Maybe the fig
Came to embrace it
So together,
They might survive

THE LITTLE PINK HOUSE

Who knows how long it has stood there along the well-traveled road. It was there when I came to the area in 1982. A small bungalow of typical Florida design. No one has ever lived there, as far as I can tell.

That cannot be true! Of course, someone built it long ago, maybe in realization of a dream. Perhaps it was a grove owners home, for it sits among sparse and fading orange trees, that at one time were lush enough to hide it from the roadside view.

Maybe, when the house was built, there was no road. Or more likely, it was a dusty lane where farm vehicles carried fruit to the packing houses. Their clatter, no doubt, flushed wild things from their sanctuary.

In later years, I imagine the dwelling may have sheltered the many transient families that worked in the groves, their very lives maneuvered by the seasons.

What are the tales, I wonder, that those aging walls might tell? I doubt the little pink house will stand much longer. Time, and the hurricanes have nibbled it away, along with the field mice and whatever else may have found refuge there.

Progress and expansion's ferocious appetite encroaches. Soon, more of old Florida will be lost forever.

CHANGING TIMES

Our home is changing
From what it was.
Time goes on and
Changes come faster
And closer

It was called "the country"
Where we live, surely
Not anymore.
There's still a horse
Or two and an orange
Grove nearby.

But widening of roads and
Industrial Parks are happening.

CIVIL WAR GHOSTS

A soft mist fell relentlessly as I stood before the stone monument that marked where a hero fell so many years ago. He gave his life for his belief in the southern cause, and though his body was not at the site, his presence was all around.

A group of rain coated buffs stood solemnly, while leaves fluttered to the ground. A guide shared his knowledge just above a whisper. As his story trailed to its end, a soft lowing was heard. Was it the fallen hero?

I had to know and shuffled through the wet leaves in the direction of the soft, mournful sound. A short distance beyond the monument was a wire fence restraining a small herd of young cattle. They were nearly alike, uniformed in faun-velvet and cream.

Large, brown eyes widened as I approached with outstretched hand, hoping to stroke a curious, moist nose. Each in unison, took one step backward, not afraid, but wary. Their eyes never left mine.

Did they know that their quiet, green pasture once roared with gunshot and ran red with blood?

HUZZAH!

He described each General and lesser officer, as if he knew them personally. He knew their height, and weight and all about their chin whiskers.

He could recite the year of their graduating West Point, as well as their class standing. He could gossip about their home life, and idiosyncrasies, and tick off the date and hour, and on which battlefield they fell.

If they did not fall, he informed us of what became of them after the "unpleasantness between the States" had accepted its fallacy.

He knew his facts and knew about fun. He shouted Huzzah, as he led us across the fields. At a museum stop, as our bus waited, and I lingered in a gift shop, a hand seized the nape of my neck, and all heard "Laggards will be shot!"

AIRPORT SECURITY

As my brother lay dying, he handed me his precious civil war bullet.

He had pried it from deep in the trunk of a tree at Manassas.

As I boarded the plane, a security search, and I with inner panic,

watched my prize examined, x-rayed and otherwise violated by the

modern world of which it had no part.

I let go my breath, when it was at last, handed back to me... my brother's treasure, now mine.

INTERRUPTIONS

A telephone ringing
Chats about nothing
The mail arrives,
--pay a bill

Grocery shopping
Enjoy a good meal
Someone's hungry,
--eat your fill

No one likes cleaning
for what is its meaning
yet it must be done,
--keep still

Joy found in reading
but TV is screaming,
can't concentrate
--sign your will

interrupted, interruption,
interrupting what?
Life?
--but this IS life

WORDLESS CONVERSATION

After so many years
Is there nothing left to say?
Or is it that we've come
To know all that's gone before.
Now, there's nothing but today.

GOD'S CREATURES

From the exotic to the most domestic, it has been a privilege to share their world. I cannot understand anyone who dislikes or fears an animal, as if they were so different from man. Man is often more to be feared. I grant, there are those, like the alligator and rattlesnake, and the man of whom it may be best to stand clear.

I have always been drawn toward animals and have experienced them in many forms. I have petted, and walked and carried, and painted animals of all kinds. I have ridden and wrestled, doctored and photographed them. I have fed, and bathed them, shared in their joyous romps and cried at their death. And never fulfilled my debt for what they have added to my life.

As I said before, ducks make me laugh. I cannot look at a duck and keep a straight face. I love their waddle and their quack, and the way they twitch their tail feathers. It delights me when a duck tilts its head to take a good look at me. I probably amuse them, too.

Many dogs and many more cats have shared my various homes. They have brought warmth and laughter and chased away my loneliness. Their unconditional love and acceptance of me, as I am, has been a priceless treasure. I wish I could live long enough to experience so many more of them, than I have, or will.

Horses have delighted me all of my life. I have never owned one and had at last to accept that I never will. But each one I encounter, as I look deeply into their lovely eyes, reaches a place inside that nothing else can touch. We should still depend on the horse for transportation.

I have ridden horses at every opportunity, but I have also ridden a camel and an elephant! When as a little girl visiting the circus grounds, I stood gazing at a tethered elephant. Suddenly, the giant very gently enfolded me in its trunk and lifted me off the ground. Just as suddenly, it carefully set me back on my feet again. Everyone gasped, including the worried trainer. I was delighted!

One summer's day I sat in a lawn chair in my mother's backyard, sipping lemonade and visiting with her. To our astonishment, a tiny blue parakeet, fluttered from the shade of a tree and perched upon my shoulder. He came home with me and stayed for a very long time.

While in the company of my fellow humans, I often observe a disinterest in the wildlife around us. Many times they don't seem to notice the seagulls, or the scampering squirrels, or the butterflies that hover nearby. As for me, I often rudely drop out of the conversation and concentrate on the critters! This world needs more critters!

TWO FOR ONE

As if of one mind
In two bodies
Sometimes they
Move, fairly slither
Across a room.
In tandem

So much alike,
How can you
Tell one from the
Other, I'm asked

Differences are there.
See the subtlety
Of movement,
And how they
Hold their feline heads

One regal, the
Other precocious

I COULD DO THAT IF I WANTED

The daily crossword nestles
Within the want-ad classifieds
My eyes are drawn to an ad;
Past and present collide.

I could do that, if I wanted
Should arrange an interview
I used to do that very same job
Though skills, I'd need renew

Would I qualify for this one,
Or maybe even that?
No, too old and satisfied
To stay home and pet my cat

DUSTING CAN WAIT

Oh my, look at the dust
But I must turn away
Many thoughts are
Beckoning today.

Dust will remain
And cover all, there's
Never any lack

But the words that
Settle on my mind --
I may not get them back.

ACTING

A stage kiss, a
Stage slap
I'm told to make
Them real.

Those two things
So hard to do
With emotion
I do not feel

LADIES, LIKE US

Elegantly dressed,
She in black velvet,
Me in black faille

A smirk, fingers dip
In champagne
A splash party is on

PHOTOGRAPH ALBUMS

There are several shelves of photograph albums in my house, and more on floors of closets. They are the big hundred page types and still they over-flow. It seems I recorded on film everybody I ever met and everything I did with them.

My little secret was that in this way, I would remember these things well into my old age. The trouble is, it isn't so. Even where I've written names in many cases, I do not remember them. Why am I posing with all those strangers?

My mother and my brother took a lot of pictures over the early years and I have inherited many of those. Neither of them ever thought to include a name or date, so most of these are lost on me.

It is kind of fun to look at old photos and see yourself grow from infant to your salad days. Growing before your eye. But no fun at all in later times to see your youth fading out and your body becoming larger.

I do enjoy reliving the good times and memories the photos have recorded. After awhile, this time-travel becomes just too bittersweet, as I close an album and return to the reality of now. It would be better if I could bring myself to throw them all away.

Andy Rooney, in one of his columns, said, "We're all trying to save our lives forever by taking pictures of it and it doesn't help."

It is the nature of photographs, especially of candid photographs, to break our hearts.

KEEP SMILING

Smile and the world
Smiles with you.
It really isn't true.

Though, I smile
at all I see,
It rarely comes
Back to me

What's worse
And so unfair is
"Good Morning"
Left hanging in air.

TEMPTATION

While our friend was away
I shed my extra pounds
Exercising, eating right,
A new lifestyle I found

Now he's back, bearing gifts;
Creamy pies, and bakery snacks.
He buys in quantity, knowing
Well, it's more than he can hack

And so it comes to me,
With love in all the sharing
I can't resist, though I insist,
I don't need all this caring!

A NEW WRINKLE

What is that, I ask myself
It wasn't there before
What's happening to
The familiar face,
I hardly know anymore?

Not creams nor wishes
Take away a lifetime
Of smiles and laughter
Nor the frowns and tears
That often followed after.

Living leaves its signature
Upon its work, well done
Taking credit for it all --
It's small payment

FAST FOOD DINING

Righteously forgoing the burger and fries, I opted for a salad, which I carried to the table on a reusable tray lined with a disposable paper place mat.

I wrestled open the clear plastic, nearly impregnable container, and reached for the Lite Vinaigrette, reduced calorie dressing. This sour little concoction was confined in a hermetically sealed foil envelope. Whoever designs such packaging, must be under the impression that people carry a scissors in their purse or pocket.

Thinking I might penetrate the foil with the flatware, I struggled nearly as much to open a plastic bag which contained knife and fork, made of what else, … plastic. These were wrapped in a paper napkin, which I added to the others that I gathered as I had passed the service area. Which, by the way, offered a variety of condiments in their little square strongholds of foil, paper and plastic.

Next I removed the plastic lid from the paper cup of diet cola, and inserted a plastic straw. The straw had to first be removed from its hygienic paper encasement. As I at last, attacked the salad, after removing the offending green peppers and added them to the pile of debris on the tray, it occurred to me that I personally had generated more than my share of refuse for the local landfill, in just one lunch.

BORROWED TIME

Spring ahead,
Then fall back --
I find it all
Confusing

Daylight saving and
Changing clocks
To me, is not
Amusing

121

CATNAPS

Playtime's ended for awhile,
Catnaps greatly needed.
Tabbies stretch out on the floor,
Their nearby toys, unheeded

EUROPEAN IMPRESSIONS

Holland:Lacy curtains, smelly cheese
Amsterdam:Live "mannequins" in windows
Germany:Black Forest cake and beer
Lucerne:Hummingbirds and crystal
Paris:Thrown out of the Ritz
Vatican:Endless stairs to stare head back
London:Bicycle confrontations there
Venice:Tilting Gondola, … thought I'd fall in
France:High-sided tub, … I fell out
Monaco:Broke the bank, a quarter in the slots
Liechtenstein:Cows have the right of way

CHOCOLATE

If you are what you eat, I must be made primarily of chocolate. Even the word, chocolate, sounds good. I've never found anything more pleasing to my taste buds than this gift from the cocoa bean.

In Belgium I devoured what I believe is the best chocolate there is, but then I haven't had time yet to taste them all! I'm working on that.

I like anything, as long as it is chocolate. Candy, cakes, pies and hot fudge sauce. Puddings and mousse are good too -- and Easter bunnies.

I honestly have tried to do without on occasion, by not bringing any chocolate home. At those times, even the semi-sweet chocolate baking bits are not safe from me.

Why fight it any longer. I say, give me chocolate or give me death. There must be chocolate in Heaven, don't you think? If not, I'll have to think twice about going.

ROLE PLAYING

Now that I've finally come to terms with who I am and ever will be, it is an embarrassment to think back to what I was. It is difficult because I was everyone and no one, for most my life.

With no faith in myself, I tried to be what others wanted me to be. Or what I supposed they wanted me to be. What an impossible task for me, and what confusion for us both.

Old habits die hard, and still come to haunt at times. It is not easy being me.

DAISY THE LITERATE

Daisy lies upon my book,
I can't see where I look
That's O.K., anyway
She's better than the book

MAKING UP IS HARD TO DO

Katie comes to visit
While, my makeup I apply
into this and into that
And all along I sigh

Ma nature gets hard to fool
as all these years go by
it doesn't help to have a cat,
its nose poked in my eye

She nudges my hands,
bats jars to the floor
runs off with the lids
to be found, nevermore

Lipstick's gone, cologne is spilled
come back with my powder puff
I love you kitty, you're so pretty,
But please, get out of my stuff!

EXPECTATION

Is that all there is?
I asked my mom --
with one foot out the door

My dear I truly hope
for you, there really
will be more

More and less was mine
as I wisely found in time,
we all must mop the floor

TYPE CAST

I learned on a manual typewriter
In my high school typing class
Those hard-clacking machines
that are now, a curiosity

My living was made on the
Electric, and the once
top-drawer Selectric

Much later, the word processor
And now, the easy touch of
a computer's keyboard

These finger have flown over
the alphabet most all
my life, to nourish my body,

and now, my soul

CORRECTIONS

The dreaded "typo"
It usually came toward
The document's end.
Crumple and start again.

Round eraser
A brush on one end.
How they tore the paper.
Crumple, and grit the teeth.

Then came chalk-treated
Paper squares.
Placed over the error,
You struck it again!
Cooler heads, wastebaskets
Less full.

Black and white ribbons
Came along,
Working in a similar way
Ah, but easier still.

Not sure in what order
"White Out" came along.
Required a light touch
Lest the results,
Be worse than the error.
There must be a better way.

Dispose of the typewriter!
Keep up with the times.
Computers, bless them,
And their miraculous
Spell-check and correct.

Blood pressure controlled!

KNOW WHAT I'M SAYING?

Ought or should
Who or that -- and
Dangling prepositions

I may not always
Get it right, but
I'll stand by my
rendition

HECK WITH SPELLCHECK

I like words like gonna,
Though they get underlined
I'm gonna use it anyway
As my writing is defined

I know I shoulda, oughta
Do what I am told,
But talk 'n rhymes, many times
Come out sounding cold.

Spell check is a handy tool
Its red lines, there to see
Dunno if it can realize,
I just wanna sound like me.

INITIAL CONFUSION

Things described with initials
Everywhere I turn,
Like S.U.V. an F.D.I.C.
I find it hard to learn

There are CD's and DVD's
Or is that BVDS?
All the same though you
Think me lame,
Spell it our for me please

There's I.R.S. and I.R.A.
Far different I am told
The more I try, -- F.Y.I.
It's more than my brain can hold

In talk today, in the U.S.A.
Full words are very few
Hard to comprehend,
I'll say it again, they're
A trial for my I.Q.

Out of sync, with this
Alphabet-ize
I am the first to confess
So in utter confusion,
Without illusion,
I'm sending an S.O.S.

TRYING TO KEEP UP

I like to read the advertising supplements in the Sunday newspaper. You know; the department stores, furniture stores, drug stores and all those wonderful coupons. I save until last, the inserts from Staples, Office Depot and other places that sell today's technical marvels.

The stuff they advertise seems to be written in another language, foreign to me. What the heck is bluetooth enabled? I thought the world was obsessed with whitening its teeth!

I pride myself a bit, that I am making the effort to live in the 21st century (the late 20th century, anyway). Trying to avoid "old fogeydom"

I have mastered much of computer usage. Who am I trying to kid? One does not master a computer. Computers have minds all their own. But at least, I plunge in and I am learning more all the time. I actually enjoy it a lot, between the moments of frustration and fury.

I use a scanner and printer with satisfaction, and I can insert a CD and listen to music while I write. I surf the net for all kinds of information and can get lost for hours on end, just "Asking Jeeves." I even play word games and piece virtual jigsaw puzzles together.

Just as I begin feeling smug, along comes another innovation, new software to master, new tips to try. But all this is only about the computer. How about all that techie stuff I see in those newspaper ads. PDA's, MP-3's, I-Pods, huh? And what about jump drive and micro vault, wireless routers, and ...oh, never mind.

I received a digital camera for Christmas. A very nice, very generous and thoughtful gift, but oh my, another door has opened. More technical stuff to study and try to absorb.

Cameras became so sophisticated, not long ago, with built-in flash and automatic film advancement. The digitals don't use film, and one doesn't even need to leave home to view and print photographs. And if you flubbed a shot, it is likely, that it can be remedied through the computer's photo editing software.

There is so much happening, so quickly, and I think I am loosing ground. Cell phones at this point for me, are only an afterthought. Don't call me, I'll call you.

ALL THERE IS ...

I am now faced with the dilemma of how to end this book, as it is a book about experiencing living. I am not ready to stop living yet, and so how do I cease the flow of thought, en massed here?

But lest my reader grow weary, I shall!

As my words have been committed to paper, I have learned, and found new insight along the way. I have tried to share that the champagne of life can be enjoyed in plastic, as thoroughly as in the best crystal.

I shall drink from this bubbly fountain of life, until besotted. Cheers!

"Sam"